THE SCIENCE OF BEING AS BEING

The Science of Being as Being

Metaphysics through Aristotle

George Couvalis

ROWMAN & LITTLEFIELD
Lanham • Boulder • New York • London

Published by Rowman & Littlefield
An imprint of The Rowman & Littlefield Publishing Group, Inc.
4501 Forbes Boulevard, Suite 200, Lanham, Maryland 20706
www.rowman.com

86-90 Paul Street, London EC2A 4NE

Copyright © 2025 by The Rowman & Littlefield Publishing Group, Inc.

All rights reserved. No part of this book may be reproduced in any form or by any electronic or mechanical means, including information storage and retrieval systems, without written permission from the publisher, except by a reviewer who may quote passages in a review.

British Library Cataloguing in Publication Information Available

Library of Congress Cataloging-in-Publication Data

Names: Couvalis, George, 1953- author.
Title: The science of being as being : metaphysics through Aristotle / George Couvalis.
Description: Lanham : Rowman & Littlefield, [2024] | Includes bibliographical references and index.
Identifiers: LCCN 2024041832 (print) | LCCN 2024041833 (ebook) | ISBN 9798881804848 (cloth) | ISBN 9798881804855 (paperback) | ISBN 9798881804862 (ebook)
Subjects: LCSH: Aristotle. Metaphysics. | Metaphysics. | Ontology.
Classification: LCC B434 .C68 2024 (print) | LCC B434 (ebook) | DDC 110.92—dc23/eng/20241022
LC record available at https://lccn.loc.gov/2024041832
LC ebook record available at https://lccn.loc.gov/2024041833

∞™ The paper used in this publication meets the minimum requirements of American National Standard for Information Sciences—Permanence of Paper for Printed Library Materials, ANSI/NISO Z39.48-1992.

THE SCIENCE OF BEING AS BEING

Metaphysics through Aristotle

GEORGE COUVALIS

ROWMAN & LITTLEFIELD
Lanham • Boulder • New York • London

Published by Rowman & Littlefield
An imprint of The Rowman & Littlefield Publishing Group, Inc.
4501 Forbes Boulevard, Suite 200, Lanham, Maryland 20706
www.rowman.com

86-90 Paul Street, London EC2A 4NE

Copyright © 2025 by The Rowman & Littlefield Publishing Group, Inc.

All rights reserved. No part of this book may be reproduced in any form or by any electronic or mechanical means, including information storage and retrieval systems, without written permission from the publisher, except by a reviewer who may quote passages in a review.

British Library Cataloguing in Publication Information Available

Library of Congress Cataloging-in-Publication Data

Names: Couvalis, George, 1953- author.
Title: The science of being as being : metaphysics through Aristotle / George Couvalis.
Description: Lanham : Rowman & Littlefield, [2024] | Includes bibliographical references and index.
Identifiers: LCCN 2024041832 (print) | LCCN 2024041833 (ebook) | ISBN 9798881804848 (cloth) | ISBN 9798881804855 (paperback) | ISBN 9798881804862 (ebook)
Subjects: LCSH: Aristotle. Metaphysics. | Metaphysics. | Ontology.
Classification: LCC B434 .C68 2024 (print) | LCC B434 (ebook) | DDC 110.92—dc23/eng/20241022
LC record available at https://lccn.loc.gov/2024041832
LC ebook record available at https://lccn.loc.gov/2024041833

∞ ™ The paper used in this publication meets the minimum requirements of American National Standard for Information Sciences—Permanence of Paper for Printed Library Materials, ANSI/NISO Z39.48-1992.

Contents

Acknowledgements   vii
Introduction   ix

1. What Is Being?   1
2. Critiques of a Science of Being   17
3. Substance, Essence and Attribute   33
4. Universals, Particulars and Dispositions   49
5. Relations   65
6. Space   81
7. Distance, Motion and Change of Place   99
8. God   115
9. The Laws of Logic   129

Epilogue   145

References   149
Index   153
About the Author   159

Acknowledgements

I would like to thank Josep Corbi, Glen Lehmann and Chris Mortensen for their support in the early stages of this work. Suzie Roux provided me with many helpful comments on various chapters. Trudi Case and Danielle Edwards provided comments and help on some chapters. Above all, I would like to thank my wife, Cheryl Simpson, for her help in many ways, and for putting up with me while I was writing.

Introduction

Metaphysics is an ancient subject and central to philosophy. However, in recent times, Metaphysics as studied by philosophers has drifted significantly from its historical roots. It is often difficult for students and professionals to find a unifying theme in books on Metaphysics. Yet everyone ought to have an accessible work on the subject that introduces it as a single unified subject. For Aristotle, whose work *Metaphysics* is one of the first systematic treatments of the subject, it is the science of being as being. I will follow Aristotle in treating Metaphysics as the science of being as being. The work called *Metaphysics* was compiled by Andronicus of Rhodes from various short texts by Aristotle and given that title because he saw it as a work that dealt with issues after the work *Physics*, also compiled by Andronicus from various short texts by Aristotle. 'Physics', as the Greeks understood it, is the study of nature in general. It is not simply Physics in the modern sense, which is a specific branch of science. Large parts of the Aristotelian texts *Physics*, *Metaphysics*, and *Categories* deal with the science of being as being. I will refer to those texts in various segments of the following chapters. My starting point in every chapter will be to present Aristotle's account and his arguments. I will also be discussing several other philosophers who deal with the same issues, ranging from Aristotle's predecessor Melissus of Samos to contemporary philosophers like Brian Ellis and David Armstrong. I will sometimes extend Aristotle's account by using other philosophers such as William of Ockham and John Locke. I will also often raise questions about Aristotle's treatment of the science of being, and sometimes reject Aristotle's arguments and conclusions.

The science of being as being seeks to distinguish the different kinds of being while also exploring the relationship between the kinds of being. As we will see, some kinds of being are dependent on other kinds of being for their existence. An example is that properties such as shape are dependent on the objects in which they are located for their existence. As we will see, there is no mystery in this fact. Such properties are simply an aspect of objects. Further, some kinds of being affect key properties of other kinds of being. For instance, the spatial distance between one object and another, which is a spatial relation, will typically affect their shapes because the gravity one object exerts on another is dependent on the distance between them.

The study of the Metaphysics of important historical figures such as Aristotle has become arcane. It has been divorced from the metaphysical debates that occur in mainstream philosophy and the philosophy of science. It is often focussed on the fine-grained analysis of the meaning of particular passages. While some historical work is important, much of it is of little interest to philosophers. In this book, I will look at forgotten insights from Aristotle and other influential philosophical figures to bear on important philosophical debates. Nevertheless, I will not be engaging in debates about interpretation. I will often also engage in significant modernisation of the views I discuss. In addition, I will take arguments out of the historical context in which they were originally produced. Much that is in Aristotle and other thinkers has been made obsolete by further argument and by the advancement of science. My Aristotle is a Neo-Aristotelian, and my Locke is a Neo-Lockean. While I will bring neglected arguments and ideas to light, this is primarily a work of philosophy not of the history of philosophy. Nevertheless, I think this work has much to offer philosophers and students of the history and philosophy of science. By bringing up often neglected views, we can see that they were important in the development of philosophy and the history of science. Many of them can be modernised to present important arguments and insights.

A key feature of Aristotle's work is that he is a kind of empiricist. He is normally reluctant to invoke entities that cannot be perceived in an everyday manner by the normal person in bright daylight. As we will see, this leads him to reject the existence of external relations between things, the existence of space and several other things. In this respect, Aristotle is an ancestor of more recent and more radical forms of empiricism. Nevertheless, Aristotle was a pioneer in the study, classification and explanation of biological organisms. These works led him to the view that living things have essences, which are crucial to explaining their behaviour and, indeed, the very existence of species. In this way, he went well beyond empiricism. We will see that the widening of Aristotle's notion of essence was a crucial part of the development of modern science and philosophy. We will also see that although Aristotle was at times willing to go well beyond a simple-minded empiricism, he was held back by his empiricism from recognising entities which play an important part in our explanations of the world. Entities such as space and relations play a crucial and ineliminable role in describing the world accurately.

Since the seventeenth century, experimental science has enormously advanced our knowledge of the world. Without going into detail about modern science, I will use insights from science at many points to comment on philosophical debates. Metaphysics has been transformed by modern science and ought to be further transformed by it. Still, we will see that we can gain important insights from Aristotle and other figures into understanding the metaphysical foundations of science, even though much of their science is obsolete.

An important insight we can gain from the development of modern science is that we can have evidence for the existence of entities and their properties which are very different from the

INTRODUCTION

entities we observe in our everyday life. Atoms, electrons and black holes are examples of some of these entities. We also have learnt from modern science that our perceptual organs are weak and subject to various illusions. Many instruments have been invented to replace our perceptual organs in detecting various aspects of the world. A simple example is that our bodies cannot tell the difference between heat and conductivity – when we enter water at the same low temperature as air, for instance, the water will feel colder. Science has also allowed us to gradually work out the crucial differences between the temperature of bodies and their specific and latent heat. Yet, as we will see, many philosophers are reluctant to introduce entities that explain features of the world in a simple and coherent manner because of empiricist prejudice, even though science has long ago gone far beyond everyday observation in explaining features of the world. Just as Aristotle introduced essences, we need a variety of entities to explain features of the world simply and coherently. Ad hoc manoeuvring to explain away various entities should not be accepted.

Throughout this work, I have avoided discussing debates about the origin of ideas. Recent research in cognitive science, cognitive psychology and philosophy has exploded simplistic views about our ideas being derived from impressions. The precise mix of innateness and experience involved is a matter of serious debate. What is no longer a matter of serious debate is that views like that of David Hume about the origin of our ideas are obsolete. This means that when I discuss Hume and the like, I will ignore arguments based on the origin of our ideas. Historians of philosophy may complain that I have ripped arguments from their context. My view is that I have saved what continues to be relevant in past philosophers. By contrast with empiricist views about the origin of our ideas, the view that our ideas should withstand the test of experiment is a powerful and important one. Where it is relevant, I have tried to take account of what has

Introduction

been established by natural science throughout this text. Where I rely on findings from natural science, I explain them and their relevance to debates in Metaphysics. However, nothing I write requires any serious knowledge of natural science.

While my discussion will cover some important metaphysical issues, it will not deal with many others. The field is far too large. This work is intended to highlight an approach that will help students and practitioners to approach issues in Metaphysics in a particular manner. It is not a survey of metaphysical issues or the final word on them.

Before I begin summarising the chapters to follow, the reader should note that throughout this work I have focussed solely on ontology. This means I am concerned with the world we encounter in our everyday life and the world science discovers. It comes in particular ways. If we want to describe it correctly, we will not be concerned with fine-grained linguistic issues, with things and properties contrived using logical devices, or with escapes from arguments about ontology using contrived formal devices. Using a phrase adapted from John Heil, this is an ontologically serious work.

In chapter one, I discuss Aristotle's view that Metaphysics is the science of being as being. I explain what Aristotle means by the phrase by comparing other sciences to the science of being as being. I present Aristotle's view that being is essence and defend it against the views of Heraclitus and Protagoras. I treat David Hume as presenting some sophisticated arguments for Heracliteanism. I argue that despite some important qualifications that need to be made to the Aristotelian view, it survives Heraclitean criticisms.

In chapter two, I turn to two kinds of criticisms of the possibility of a science of being as being. The first kind originates in the arguments of Aquinas that being and essence are distinct. The second originates in the arguments of Hume that existence is not a property, and of Bertrand Russell that existence is a property of statements and not of things. I will then turn to neglected arguments from William of Ockham to argue that Aquinas is wrong because he is confusing descriptions and things. I also argue that Hume and Russell are misled by their extreme empiricism into thinking that if existence is a property, it must be a directly perceivable property. Still, I argue that Ockham does not explain how we come to have the notion of things existing external to our minds. I suggest that the best explanation is to be found in Kant's view that the notion is innate – we bring it to experience, we do not get it from experience.

In chapter 3, I set out Aristotle's view in *Categories*, which I understand to be setting out the various kinds of being and some relations between them. I will then turn to an exposition of the notions of substance, essence and attribute. I argue that substance is to be identified with essence. I then turn to giving an exposition of the notion of essence. I argue that essences are to be identified with causal powers or capacities. Attributes are to be identified with the interaction of the causal powers of things with things external to them. I use not only arguments that can be found in the Aristotelian tradition but a knowledge of some key features of modern science.

In chapter 4, I discuss whether some essences and attributes are to be understood to be universals which are multiply instantiated, rather than particulars. Crucial parts of Aristotle's *Metaphysics* seem to argue for the view that there are multiply instantiated universals in the world. This view has been taken up by recent philosophers who argue that there are categorical properties, and that laws of nature are to be best understood as relations between universals. I argue that there are no good reasons for believing in the existence of universals. Universals are not an addition to being, and they do not explain scientific laws. Scientific laws are to be explained through the causal powers of things, not through the universals they supposedly instantiate.

INTRODUCTION

In chapter 5, I turn to a discussion of whether relations exist in addition to things involved in relations. An ancient view is that relations are not beings in addition to the beings which are related. This view, which is to be found in Aristotle and many medieval philosophers, was vigorously challenged by Bertrand Russell. Recently, however, a number of philosophers have argued that though some relational statements are true and have accepted that Russell provided important insights into the logic of relations, relations do not exist in addition to what is being related. I argue that while some relations do not exist in addition to the things related, other relations exist in addition to the things related, but not independently of them. This means that Russell was right in thinking that relations are genuine and irreducible additions to being.

In chapter 6, I discuss space. I start by discussing Aristotle's view that space does not exist because there is a plenum of material objects with nothing in between them. I then turn to setting out John Philoponus's arguments that space exists as a separate thing, the three-dimensional, and his criticisms of Aristotle. I continue by discussing the arguments of Leibniz and his followers that space is constituted out of the relations between things. Leibniz intended to modernise and defend Aristotle's anti-realism about space. I argue that the most plausible hypothesis is that space exists as a thing in which other things are located. Indeed, some of their properties are transformed by space. This makes the study of its features a central addition to the science of being.

In chapter 7, I discuss the nature of space, material objects and changes. I start, like Aristotle, by considering some of Zeno's paradoxes, which seem to have been intended to present a case for two claims: first, that there is no separation between things, and second, that change and motion are impossible. I then present Aristotle's arguments that Zeno's mistakes result from his assumption that motion, time, and material objects consist of an infinite number of items of no size. Aristotle argues that these do not consist of an infinite number of items of no size, but of intervals which can be broken down indefinitely into other intervals. I then turn to the standard modern accounts of denseness and continuity, which treat time, space and material objects as consisting of an infinite number of points in an order. Overall, although I recognise this view as consistent, I find it implausible and Aristotle's view more defensible. Standard modern accounts are to be treated as convenient mathematical devices for solving problems rather than realistic representations of the world.

In chapter 8, I consider some arguments for the existence of God or gods. I situate the arguments for the existence of gods in Aristotle's inability to explain the movements in the heavens and on earth through the causal powers of natural things. I also situate the arguments for the existence of gods in the inability of the ancients to explain biological order. I argue, following Hume and some recent philosophers, that arguments for the existence of gods are inconclusive. There is no good evidence that there is a god or gods, though there are important problems that remain unaccounted for about the origin of the universe. Gods do not merit further study as a kind of being.

In chapter 9, I discuss Aristotle's argument that there are laws of being, the logical laws of non-contradiction and excluded middle. I explain why Aristotle thinks that these are laws of being, and not merely conceptual principles. I go through some of Aristotle's key arguments for these principles as well as some important criticisms of Aristotle's arguments. I argue that Aristotle has failed to establish that the law of excluded middle is a universal truth. There may be marginal cases of things that are transitional between two kinds that do not obey excluded middle. This means that the account of essences may need to be qualified. Even so, as I explain, Aristotle's account is roughly correct. Aristotle is also correct in thinking of such principles as laws of being. After discussing the case of excluded middle, I turn to a recent argument that our phenomenology does not obey the law of non-contradiction. I argue that this argument is correct and that it raises the possibility that the law of non-contradiction may not be true in reality.

In the Epilogue, I consider briefly three other parts of Metaphysics that will be illuminated by Aristotle's approach, arguments and solutions. They are the nature of time, the nature of numbers, and the nature of intentionality. I also suggest that there may be further Aristotelian contributions to metaphysics.

Throughout this work, I have added key references to the views I discuss at the end of each chapter rather than throughout the text. The solutions proposed to problems in metaphysics can be stated without the careful analysis of texts. Arguments can usually be stated more clearly without focussing on details. My references to Plato, Aristotle and Kant also include references to the standard editions of their works. Readers who do not use my translations can use another translation. If they read the original languages, they can read the text in those languages.

CHAPTER 1

What Is Being?

Let us start with the ancient Greek philosopher Aristotle. In the group of texts called *Metaphysics*, he focusses on a single claim. It occurs in its clearest form at the beginning of Book Gamma (book 4; there are two books Alpha). He declares that '[T]here is a science which investigates being as being and the attributes that belong to it through its own nature' (Ross 1928, 1003a 20).

What does he mean by this obscure remark? On his account, Metaphysics deals with what exists, that is, everything. It is not, however, a list of all the things that exist. Listing my cat, my mobile phone and the other things in the universe would be useless to Metaphysics. Neither is it an aggregate of the various sciences which deal with kinds of things. Biology, Chemistry and Physics are of importance to Metaphysics, but they are not Metaphysics. Biology, for instance, deals with living things as living things, not as beings. Physics might be thought to be the fundamental science because it deals with the fundamental components of everything, as well as with the laws that govern those components. Nevertheless, Physics only deals with certain properties of things, such as their mass. It does not deal with them as beings. Aristotle thinks that the natural sciences do not deal with a different and broader question which deals with everything, which is, what is being?

Chapter 1

To answer this question, Aristotle thinks that we need to construct what he calls an 'episteme' of being, a science of being. He does not mean by this that it is a science in the sense that Biology is a science. It does not involve doing experiments on being, or systematic observation of it. While observations lie in the background of discussions of being, a science of being is, rather, a systematic study of beings as beings. Just as Biology deals with the various kinds of living things as living things, the study of being deals with beings as beings. Biology seeks to classify the different kinds of living things into genera and species and identify their peculiarities as living things. Only the aspects of other sciences relevant to Biology are studied by biologists. For instance, Biology only deals with the aspects of physics relevant to living things as living things geared to survive and reproduce. Similarly, Metaphysics does not in any detail deal with living and non-living things as living or non-living things; instead, it deals with them as beings.

Using a phrase invented by one of the ancient editors of Aristotle's works, the question what is being? deals with Metaphysics, in which 'meta' means 'beyond', and 'physics' means the study of nature in all its manifestations: biological, chemical, geological and so on. Metaphysics deals with items beyond in the sense that they are more fundamental, not in the sense that it only deals with spooky things that are not natural objects. To understand the ways in which they are more fundamental, we need to grasp two points: (1) Aristotle identifies being with existence. He thinks that the question 'what is being?' is fundamental because we are seeking to explain what makes the various existing things existing things. (2) Aristotle thinks that the aspects of beings discussed by the various natural sciences and in everyday life come in broad kinds, such as substance and its attributes, which cut across various natural sciences. If Aristotle is right, what is being? is the fundamental question of Metaphysics. For the moment, we will focus on the first point. The notions of substance, attribute and so on, will be explained and discussed in detail in a later chapter.

Why Being?

Let me start with a strange question. We often talk about things which we merely fancy to exist or hallucinate as existents. Suppose I hallucinate my long-deceased cat, Pushkin, to be in the corner of the room. But apparently, she is not there, as she died long ago. What is it that would make it true that Pushkin is there? What is it for Pushkin to exist as opposed to not existing? Considering this question will allow us to better understand point 1.

One possible answer is nothing. There is no difference between vividly and persistently hallucinating that there is a cat and the existence of a cat. Although this view is startling, Aristotle thought it was the view of the Greek philosopher Protagoras.

Protagoras's View

In *Metaphysics Gamma*, Aristotle proceeds in part by criticising the Greek philosopher Protagoras. For Protagoras, every perception is equally true. If I perceive that a ship is approaching, and you perceive that no ship is approaching, we must both be right.

Protagoras's view seems to have been more complex than I have just described. He seems to have thought that all beliefs whatsoever were equally true. Protagoras seems to have arrived at his view through the observation that different groups of people had different beliefs about what is true and what is false. What is regarded as true in Athens is often not regarded as true among the Persians, and so on. Anthropological studies seem to show that people have a wide variety of beliefs about many aspects of the world. The believers in different groups often seem to believe that they are without a doubt correct in their beliefs. This seems to be the reason why many modern Protagoreans hold Protagoras's view.

CHAPTER 1

CRITICISMS OF PROTAGORAS'S VIEW

Now it is fairly easy to see that we cannot go logically from anthropological studies to the conclusion that all beliefs (or perceptions) are equally true. It may be that some beliefs are true and others are not, whatever the views of the believers. It is also clearly possible that some beliefs are held by people who have not subjected those beliefs to a serious test. Someone who believes that machine gun bullets or very high doses of radioactivity will not kill them can easily be shown to have false beliefs. People who believe what the perception of mirages in the desert seem to tell them are likely to die. So, mere difference in commonly accepted beliefs between communities does not show that Protagoras is right. Indeed, the obvious fact that some beliefs can be easily shown to be wrong shows that Protagoras is wrong.

Before Aristotle, Plato pointed out that the belief that all beliefs are equally true leads to some additional problematic results. We can state his point in a modern manner. Many people in many societies do not believe that all beliefs are equally true. If all beliefs are equally true, then, suppose someone believes that not all beliefs are equally true, this must be as true as Protagoras's belief. Protagoras propounded his view as if it were a universal truth. But if the view is a universal truth, it has the consequence that it cannot be a universal truth. In response to this problem, followers of Protagoras could try to say that Protagoras's view is different from other views. It is somehow exalted above them so that if there is a conflict, it is true and the other views are not. However, if they say this without any argument, they can be reasonably ignored. They have presented no evidence for the claim that Protagoras's view is superior to the ordinary view that some beliefs are true and others are false.

There is, however, another way in which Protagoras's view can be understood. It can be understood to be saying that whatever someone believes to be true is true *for the believer*. While this would allow Protagoras to escape from the objection in the previous paragraph, it is very implausible. People often find that their beliefs are false and change their minds. Beliefs and perceptions can be shown to be wrong in everyday practical ways, as we have seen in the example of the mirage discussed earlier. So even those who have a particular belief can later realise that they have no good ground for the belief.

It is possible for someone to modify Protagoras's view by arguing that everyday beliefs about the world can be obviously true or false, as can certain beliefs about matters of natural science, but that other beliefs such as ethical beliefs or beliefs about supernatural entities cannot be shown to be true or false. Perhaps Protagoras's view can continue to be maintained about such beliefs. Once again, however, the mere fact that beliefs about ethics or about supernatural entities cannot be shown decisively to be true or false does not mean that the believers of those beliefs are all correct, or correct to themselves. It is logically compatible with a wide diversity of beliefs on these matters that everyone is wrong, or that some are wrong and some are right. Further argument beyond the diversity of beliefs is required to show that Protagoras is right about these sorts of beliefs. I will not take up this issue here. It is sufficient for my purposes that Protagoras is wrong about many everyday beliefs and many scientific beliefs.

HERACLITUS'S VIEW

Now consider another view. The Greek philosopher Heraclitus thought, for good reason, that everything is changing. Everything is like a river. We might not be able to perceive the changes because they are very small. Still, they are happening. Heraclitus is supposed to have put this view by saying that we cannot step into the same river twice. His follower, Cratylus, is supposed to have argued that we cannot step into the same river even once. The reason is that the river is changing as we are stepping into it. To modernise Heraclitus's thought, we might think of the fact that a material object like my computer is made up of tiny atoms. In every time interval, however short, my computer is losing a number of atoms, or is in the process of losing a number of atoms. Parts of it are also reacting chemically with oxygen and other gases in the surrounding air. So, things are also being added to it. This seems to mean that even when I am thinking about something, like the computer on which I am writing this, I cannot refer to the same thing. Thought takes time and whatever it is I am thinking about will have changed into something else as I am thinking. As I think the thought 'the computer in front of me', the computer has been replaced by something else. No wonder that Aristotle says that Cratylus was in the end reduced to inarticulately wiggling his finger rather than saying anything.

Hume's Modern Cratyleanism

In the eighteenth century, David Hume expanded on the arguments Aristotle ascribed to Cratylus. Hume thought that all that was available to us is experience and the contents of experience. All talk that is not based on experience is unwarranted or downright incoherent. He claimed that, strictly speaking, something complex can only retain its identity when every part of it remains the same (Hume 2007, 167). What he meant was that every part of it remains the same as it was at a particular time. He argued that, on this criterion, everything we know changes to some degree, but when we do not notice the changes, or notice them very little, we are inclined to think that we are dealing with exactly the same thing. Thus, when small parts of a mountain change, we call it the same mountain. By contrast, when a small stone has a clearly visible part broken off it, we are likely to think the stone no longer exists. Similarly, when the parts of something change slowly over time, we think of it as the same thing. An ancient puzzle illustrates the point: The ship of the Greek king Theseus gradually changes plank by plank until not a single piece of wood in it is the same. Yet we would be inclined to call it the same thing. In addition, when something is used for the same purpose as its predecessor in the same place, we are apparently inclined to call it the same thing. A church with a particular name can be burnt down and replaced by a new building, but we call it the same church. Hume noted that when something has many parts that work together to a common end, such as in vegetables or animals, then we are inclined to ascribe a continuing identity to them. Even when something has grown from a small plant into a tree, and all of its parts have been replaced over time, we apparently think of it as the same thing. Hume then turned to his own mind and argued for the same conclusion. He was thinking of the rapid changes in his own perceptions, but the point can also be made about his material self. Even while Hume is thinking, small particles of his body are leaving it, and others are replacing them.

To see the power of Hume's line of argument, consider that many particles in you were added to you over your lifetime and many particles have left every part of your body over your lifetime. After all, you were once a very small infant. You have changed radically over time; yet you talk as if you are the same individual you once were.

Unlike Cratylus, Hume may well have been intending to bring out the sceptical absurdities of his train of thought while being unable to deal with the problem he raised.

Criticisms of Heraclitus's View

Aristotle's great predecessor, the Greek philosopher Plato, argued that Cratylus's view means that nothing is anything in itself – nothing has any being in itself:

> *The upshot of all this is that . . . we should exclude 'be' from everywhere . . . nor ought we admit 'something', 'someone's', 'my', 'this', 'that', or any word that brings things to a standstill. We ought, rather, to use expressions that conform to the nature of things, and speak of them as coming to be, undergoing production, ceasing to be and altering: because if anyone brings*

Chapter 1

> *things to a standstill by what he says, he'll be easy to refute in doing that, and we ought to speak that way both about individual cases and about numbers of things taken together in collections, to which people apply the name man, stone or any animal or kind of thing. (Plato 1973, 24; 157b-c)*

On this account, I cannot think about my cat Pushkin without her being replaced by another object as I am thinking. Of course, Cratylus's view also undermines the idea that there is an I that is thinking about things. As thought takes time, the I that is supposed to be thinking has changed into something else.

Plato drew a startling conclusion from Cratylus's view, which is

> *if all things do change, then every answer, whatever it's about, is equally correct: both that things are so and that they're not so, or if you like, both that they come to be so, and that they come to be not so, so as not to bring these people to a standstill by what we say . . . one oughtn't even to use this word 'so' because what's so wouldn't any longer be changing. (Plato 1973, 63-4; 183a-b)*

Cratylus's view implies that we cannot think or talk correctly about anything. Indeed, its implications run even deeper. Cratylus's view also applies to us. As we are also changing all of the time, there is no one to think the thoughts we apparently have. But it seems that we are persistent beings who do have coherent thoughts about the world and that some objects we think about are fairly stable.

There is, perhaps, a qualification to be made to Plato's argument. According to some philosophers, such as Bertrand Russell, time consists of instants of zero size. While this view is startling, logicians and mathematicians believe that they have shown that it is a coherent view. I will discuss this startling view further in a later chapter. In any case, thought takes some non-zero time, so Plato's argument is still strong.

Plato's Diagnosis and Aristotle's Solution

Both Protagoras's view and the Cratylean view seem to lead to serious problems. We can no longer be a thinking or talking subject who thinks correctly or coherently about anything on these views. Yet it seems that we are such subjects as can be seen by the fact that we understand their arguments and try to respond to them. Why are they wrong?

Plato's remarks about Cratylus give us a hint. Both Protagoras and Cratylus have made us exclude 'be' from descriptions of the world. What is going wrong is that some fairly persistent things exist in the world whether we represent them as existing or not. But what does this mean? Aristotle thinks this question has a very simple answer. For something to exist is for it to have a nature in itself independently of any perception. It is, in his phraseology, an 'itself through itself'. For something to be an itself through itself, there must be something that it is to be that thing. What it is to be that thing must be, to some extent persistent for us to be able to identify things in the world and talk about them.

Let us return to my example of hallucinating a cat as opposed to a real cat being present to clarify Aristotle's answer. Aristotle thought that there is not a what it is to be a hallucinated cat; whereas in the case of seeing a cat, there would be a what it is to be that cat. A hallucinated cat is only a representation of a cat in our heads, which is deceptive. Whatever makes a cat real is the what it is to be of a cat. Aristotle thought that what makes a cat what it is, is its substance (or its substratum). It is its substance that gives its characteristic causal powers and liabilities; that is, it is its substance that constitutes the intrinsic features which explain how it develops and how it interacts with other things. The cat will have less fur in summer and more fur in winter. It is constantly shedding fur and adding fur. As it ages, some of its fur may fall out, and it may develop bald patches. Nevertheless, it is the same substance until it dies. The point of using the metaphor of a substratum for what something is over time is that the foundations of a house, its substratum, are hidden from plain sight; however, they exist and hold up the house while it exists. Many of the superficial visible features of the house can change over time while we call it the same house. Similarly, the characteristic powers and liabilities of a cat, as well as its pattern of growth and decay, are to be explained by something in it which is the cause of its properties.

We might ask, however, what exactly is the substance of something like a cat? Aristotle identifies being a substance with having an essence. On his account, without essences, there would be no external world and no persistent things. There could be no themselves in virtue of themselves. Essences constitute things. They are what they are, and it is because of them that they have their characteristic powers and liabilities. What exists outside of our minds must either have an essence, be dependent on the essence of a thing, or be made up of things that have an essence. Aristotle's Biology has long been obsolete. But his basic line of argument remains plausible. Modern biologists might identify being a cat with having certain active DNA. I will leave aside whether this is the right answer, as, in my view, the nature of the essence of a particular kind of thing is to be determined by science. Metaphysics cannot answer that question.

Let us see in more detail how Aristotle's answer might deal with the problems raised by Cratylus and Protagoras. A cat can be a persistent cat even though it develops from an embryo to a kitten and then to an adult cat. All the time, it is eating and excreting. It is gaining particles and losing them. Nevertheless, it continues to be that cat. There is a pattern in its development and its behaviour. It has characteristic powers and liabilities at various stages of its life. It can eat certain kinds of food and convert them into part of its body. It can climb and sneak up on its prey. It can be injured by certain kinds of bacteria and viruses. All of this ceases when the cat dies. None of these features are dependent on how the cat is perceived or what we believe about it. I might believe that the cat is the ball of fluff and try to treat it as such only to be scratched and bitten by it.

Now consider something else. The things that exist apparently include not only things, but properties of those things as well. I am a certain height and a certain weight. On Aristotle's account, those properties are not essential properties. They do not make me what I am. I can lose weight, and, when I was much younger, I was much shorter. What about such properties? Are they also themselves in virtue of themselves? Apparently not. My height and weight seem to be, at least in part, due to intrinsic genetic features of me. They are, of course, also due to other things in the world, such as what I ate when I was young. Properties such as height and weight are accidental properties for Aristotle. In saying this, it is important to emphasise that Aristotle does not mean that it is a complete coincidence that these properties inhere in things. Rather, it seems that he thinks that they are caused by the interaction of the essential properties of a thing with other things in the world. They are attributes things have at a particular stage of their existence.

Responses to Hume's Argument

While I have given the reader some reasons to think that Aristotle can adequately respond to Protagorean and Cratylean arguments, I have not, so far, dealt adequately with Hume's arguments. An Aristotelian would have to concede some points to Hume while rejecting other claims.

The first claim that an Aristotelian would reject is that something that changes in its minutest part is not the same thing as it was before the change. Hume assumes that all things that exist are mere collections of parts. On the contrary, some things have inherent in them something which causes them to transform things they consume into functioning parts of themselves. Human beings, trees and many other things are things which have in them an inherent tendency to change in particular ways over time in order to function as unities. To say that they are the same thing is to say that the structure of the thing develops in a predictable way over time due to its essence. The same human being does not consist of the same parts. A human being is a structured organism that has a spatiotemporal history in which it changes from an embryo to an adult and then decays. It is not a mere collection of parts.

Hume is, however, partly right about some other things. A mountain is a collection of parts, and to treat mountains as single unitary things over time is a useful convention because their parts do not change much over time by comparison to the whole and it is convenient to treat them as if they were unchanging wholes for practical purposes. Nevertheless, the parts of mountains are persistent things that have being. That is why planes sometimes crash into mountains even if their pilots think they are flying safely. A mountain at a time is a real thing consisting of parts, and for many practical purposes, it does not matter that it is constantly changing. We can say similar things about rivers and many other things we encounter in our everyday lives.

Let me note, however, that there some further problems with Hume's Cratyleanism concerning mountains, rivers and other such things. While there is no science that deals with the essences of mountains, rivers, and the like, geographers and geomorphologists find it useful to treat them as entities that have a history and change in systematically describable ways over time. By focussing on minute changes, we can fail to note real patterns in the way in which these things behave on a larger scale, in which minute differences are irrelevant. In this way, these things are not as radically unlike human beings or trees as we might think. Hume fails to note that our treatment of aspects of the world is not merely because of a kind of myopia, but because we can notice real patterns in the world at various scales. To have being, such entities must consist of parts that are more robust than they are, though they are not mere aggregates of these parts. So, there is a sense in which even mountains and rivers have being diachronically. They have being over time as real patterns consisting of materially changing parts, even if they do not have an essence that produces those patterns.

Hume is also right to say that we treat human artefacts such as ships as the same, even though we can change them a little at a time by repairing them until not a single part is the same in the end. In such cases, the fact that they serve the same purpose in much the same way leads us to call them the same thing, even though there is no internal factor causing them to have a life history. However, against Hume's conclusion that ships do not exist diachronically, it should be said that our repairing them and using them for the same purpose is a kind of substitute for having an internal cause of unity and continuity. An external cause, our activities in repairing them to carry out an end, gives them unity and continuity. Further, note that an individual ship also has a spatiotemporal history that is continuous, even if its parts do not have such a history. This is why we distinguish, for instance, between the Australian navy ship HMAS Adelaide (I) and the current ship with the same name, HMAS Adelaide (III). So, on balance, we have some reason for saying that human artefacts that we repair and which carry out the same purpose in much the same way are the same thing. Their unity is not provided by the specific parts, but by the purpose they fulfil, the fact that they fulfil their purpose in much the same way, and their continuous spatiotemporal history. Once again, we do not have an aggregate of parts, but something in which the parts function together in a particular manner for a particular end. Of course, ships and the like do not have an essence, and their parts must be robust in order to fulfil the purpose for which they are designed.

What about churches and other institutional entities? Hume is certainly right to say that a new church that is very different in the kinds of materials it is made of can replace an older building yet still be treated as if it is the same church. A wooden church of Saint Andrew can be replaced by a sandstone church of Saint Andrew in roughly the same place. A church that is not the same building can be thought of as the same church. Yet here too, we are not just deluded. A church is both a building and an institutional entity. As an institutional entity, it can continue to be the same church while it is not the same building. It is used for the same purposes in roughly the same place and dedicated to the same saint. Hume's argument muddles the institutional entity with the building. Of course, if the same, or much the same, building is used for a quite different purpose, it ceases to be the institutional entity that it once was. The Parthenon in Athens, originally a pagan temple to the goddess Athena, became a Christian church. As a pagan temple, it ceased to exist while it continued to exist as a building. Its remains are now a museum piece and a tourist attraction, and not a pagan temple.

The key problem with Hume's argument is that he treats all things as mere aggregates of parts and introduces the claim, as if it were obvious, that our idea of identity means that the parts of a thing must be unchanging. As can be seen from my discussion, it is far from obvious that our idea of identity is the idea of mere aggregates, or, more importantly, that things in the world are mere aggregates. Nevertheless, Hume is correct about one thing. Both in cases where there is an underlying cause of the unity of a thing and in cases where there is not, minor changes are treated by us as irrelevant, and what counts as a minor change depends on our perception and the object perceived. If a large mountain on a planet disappeared and was dispersed into space due to a meteorite collision, we would still call it the same planet. Judgements of the continuing identity of things are partly dependent on human perceptions and human interests. This means that our notions of identity and diversity are, in part, pragmatic.

I have pointed out some strengths of Hume's line of argument as well as various problems with it. It is important to mention that while only some of the entities I have discussed have essences, modern Aristotelians are committed to arguing that the other things can only exist at a time if they are composed of parts that have essences. Mountains, ships and churches are dependent for their existence on things which have essences. While Aristotle rejected atomism, a modern Aristotelian might say, for example, that in a ship largely made of iron, the iron atoms have an essence which gives the ship many of its characteristic features. A ship cannot be composed of things that do not have essences. This means that the central thesis of Aristotelianism, that the being of all things is dependent on things which have essences, survives Humean criticisms.

Conclusion

I have presented some preliminary arguments for Aristotle's claim that there is a science of being. I have also argued that the being of things is to be identified with the substance of those things, or with the substances that make them up. In addition, I have presented a preliminary argument for the claim that the substance of a thing should be identified with its essence. In a later chapter, I will discuss some debates about substance and essence in detail. I will also discuss attributes in detail. However, as I have noted, Hume's discussion of identity shows up some important features of our everyday talk. Many things we talk about do not have an essence, although they consist of things that have essences.

Further Readings

An important defence of a science of being is contained in Aristotle's *Metaphysics*, Book Gamma (Book 4; there are two books Alpha: Alpha major and Alpha the lesser). Chapters one and two of Gamma set out Aristotle's initial case for a science of being. An excellent translation and introduction, which also contains explanatory notes on the text, is Reeve 2016. Ross 1928 is the classic translation but lacks notes. Politis 2004 is a very useful work which explains key features of Aristotle's text. Chapter 4 discusses Aristotle's initial arguments for a science of being in some detail. I have covered a part of Aristotle's later discussion in *Gamma* through my discussion of Heraclitus and Protagoras. However, much of the argument in the later part of *Gamma* relies on a defence of the principles of non-contradiction and excluded middle. I will discuss that defence in more detail in a later chapter.

David Hume's *Of Personal Identity*, which is a chapter in his *Treatise of Human Nature* (Hume 2007, 164–170), contains many interesting arguments about identity and is very clear and easy to understand. While the focus is on personal identity, which I do not cover here, much of the discussion is about identity in general. Some of Hume's argument relies on an untenable and radical empiricism. I have no space to discuss that empiricism here. I take it to have been shown to be radically deficient.

Plato's dialogue *Theaetetus* presents and criticises the views of Protagoras and Heraclitus in some detail. The views of Protagoreans and Heracliteans are presented by various characters, and Socrates criticises their views. Sections 170a – 171e and 180d – 183c contain the key discussions. A very useful commentary and analysis is Burnyeat 1990. The text also contains M. J. Levett's fine translation of the *Theaetetus*.

CHAPTER 2

Critiques of a Science of Being

Some philosophers have thought that the identification of the being of a thing with its essence is mistaken. They have argued that a study of the things that exist is separate from the study of essences. Other philosophers have challenged the very notion of a systematic study of being, which is separate from particular sciences. They have thought that such a notion is a conceptual mistake. On their account, those who talk about a systematic study of being are treating being as a property, or something like a property. Such talk is radically mistaken. Talking about existence is really talking about the properties of linguistic or conceptual items, not of items in the world.

AQUINAS'S CRITICISM
In the thirteenth century, Thomas Aquinas criticised Aristotle's identification of being with essence. He put forth a very simple argument. We can understand what something is independently of whether it exists or not. Thus, something can have an essence whether it exists or not. If it has an essence, then we can make true statements about it even if it does not exist. To understand Aquinas's point, consider a sentence about something that does not yet exist but will exist. Take a cat that will come into existence next year. Call her Isobel. The statement referring to Isobel, 'the

cat is a cat' seems to be obviously true. But how can it be obviously true if the essence of the cat is identical with the cat, or some key feature of the cat; for the cat does not yet exist? Now, it might be thought that Aquinas's argument can be evaded by arguing that a cat-essence is some kind of universal thing that already exists. But the point can be put without presupposing the existence of any cats. Take the time before cats existed. Think of Isobel. At that time, it could have apparently been correct to think that 'the cat is a cat' (even if only an all-knowing god could have thought the sentence). Similarly, at that time, it seems that 'the essence of the cat is an essence' must be true.

Ockham's Response to Aquinas's Argument

William of Ockham responded to the above argument by arguing that it is mistaken. His argument amounts to this: 'The cat is a cat', indexed to the time before cats existed, is false, as is 'the essence is an essence', since the subject of the sentences does not yet exist. The subject of the sentences is nothing at the time. Presumably, this also means that even 'cats are cats', indexed to the time before cats existed, is false. Cats were nothing at that time, so no statement referring to them could be true.

At first sight, Ockham's response seems bizarre. Surely, we might think, 'cats are cats' is necessarily true even when indexed to a time when cats do not exist. But Ockham's point can be spelt out by distinguishing between the description of the essence of cats and the cats themselves. It may be possible to describe the essence of cats before cats exist – perhaps their essence is a particular kind of DNA, for instance. Let's call the essence X. Then it will be true that the description of X is the description of X. But this is trivial. For a statement like 'the description of a golden mountain is the description of a golden mountain' is true even though there are no golden mountains at any time, and non-existent golden mountains do not have an essence; so that their essence cannot be distinct from their existence. Aquinas is confusing a description or a concept with the item the concept may or may not denote in the world. An essence is something in the external world, not a concept. So, 'cats are cats' is false when we are using the sentence to refer to things in the world at a time when there were no cats. Similarly, 'the essence is an essence' when we are referring to cats as things in the world is false when cats do not yet exist.

HUME'S AND RUSSELL'S CRITICISM

In the eighteenth century, David Hume put the central modern criticism of a property of being very clearly when he argued that if we have an idea of existence as such or external existence as such (existence outside of our own minds), we must have an idea derived from some experienced impression. However, when we conceive of a thing and then conceive of it existing, there is no experienced difference at all. 'The idea of existence, then, is the very same as the idea of what we conceive to be existent . . . That idea, when conjoin'd with the idea of any object, makes no addition to it' (Hume 2007, 48). In a letter in which Hume replies anonymously to the critics of his *Treatise of Human Nature*, he adds:

> [O]ur author indeed asserts . . . that we have no abstract or general ideas, properly so speaking; and that those ideas, which are called general, are nothing but particular ideas fixed to general terms. Thus, when I think of a horse in general, I must always conceive that horse as black or white, fat or lean, etc. and can form no notion of a horse that is not of some particular colour or size. In prosecution of the same topic the author hath said, that we have no general Idea of existence, distinct from every particular existence. (Hume 2007, 428)

In the early twentieth century, Bertrand Russell was so impressed by Hume's argument that we have no general idea of existence that he stated, '[S]o long as it was thought that "existence" . . . could be significantly predicated of an actual given particular, it was impossible to answer Hume's contention that existence adds nothing to the subject' (Russell 1913, 138–39).

One thing that underlies Hume's and Russell's thinking is the view that if existence is a property, it must be a distinguishing property. Hume and Russell are both strong empiricists about our concepts of objects in the external world. That is, they both think that our concepts of external objects and their parts are derived from experience. They believe that this has the absurd consequence that if existence is some sort of property of objects in the external world, an existing thing must appear different from a non-existent thing, even though there are no non-existent things. Russell explains the point through a joke:

> *it is obvious that, if you think of the things there are in the world, they cannot be divided into two classes – namely those that exist and those that do not. Non-existence is, in fact, a very rare property. Everyone knows the story of the two German pessimistic philosophers of whom one exclaimed: 'How much happier were it never to have been born'. To which the other replied with a sigh: 'True! But how few are those who achieve this happy lot'.* (Russell 1956, 137)

Hume and Russell's point is well taken; however, their extreme empiricism leads them to neglect the possibility that being is a universal property of things and not a distinguishing property.

As the second quote from Hume above indicates, he also thinks that our ideas of things must be precise in every way because we get them through specific impressions; though by attaching them to general terms, we enable them to stand for a number of things which differ in various ways. We will see later in this chapter that Ockham gives us a good reason to doubt this claim.

In a very influential account, Russell tried to explain how we could talk significantly about existence by saying that any properly understood statement '. . . exists' has the logical form 'there is an x, such that x is a. . .'. He called the logical form 'x is a . . . ' 'a propositional function' when the ' . . . ' is filled in by some predicate. For instance, 'unicorn'. He said that

> [E]xistence is essentially a property of a propositional function. It means that the propositional function is true in at least one instance. If you say 'There are unicorns', that will mean 'There is an x, such that x is a unicorn'. (Russell 1918, 204)

The statement 'there is an x such that. . .' picks out the things in the world and attributes a predicate to at least one of them. If at least one of them really has the property attributed to it by the predicate, the statement will be true. If none of them have the property, the statement will be false. Unicorns don't exist because there is nothing in the world having the property of being a unicorn. So, on Russell's account, existence is a property of propositional functions, not of things. This is how he thought we could solve Hume's problem.

Russell was initially led to propose his propositional function account by thinking about statements in mathematics, such as there is an even number in the series of natural numbers between 2 and 6. That statement is true because there is such a number, namely 4. At the time Russell first thought of his propositional function account, he thought that we had access to a world of mathematical objects, so he interpreted the statement about the even number as a claim about the existence of that number.

Discussion of Russell's Solution

Unfortunately, however, Russell's propositional function account does not solve the problem Aristotle was addressing, for it does

CHAPTER 2

not indicate what makes things things (what makes beings beings), which is what Aristotle wanted to know. On the contrary, it makes it entirely mysterious what makes something an inhabitant of the external world as opposed to the object of a hallucination. In some of his work, Russell tried to bite the bullet on this and to make the objects of hallucinations real. He thought that phantoms and images are not fundamentally different from external objects except that

> *[I]f you shut your eyes and imagine a visual scene and you stretch out your hand to touch what is imaged, you won't get a tactile sensation, or even necessarily a tactile image. You will not get the usual correlation of sight and touch . . . The general correlations of your images are quite different from what one chooses to call 'real' objects. But that is not to say that such images are unreal, it is only to say that they are not part of Physics.*

He went on to give a similar account of Macbeth's Dagger

> *Macbeth sees a dagger. If he tried to touch it, he would not get any tactile sensation, but that does not imply he was not seeing a dagger, it only implies that he was not touching it. It does not in any way imply that the visual impression was not there. (Russell 1918, 224)*

Russell's view of external existents is a form of what is called 'neutral monism' in which the view of one perceiver is supplemented by the views of others, and in which psychological phenomena are explained by different laws to physical phenomena. Nevertheless, the components of the psychological and the physical world are the same kind of thing – this is why neutral monism is a monism which is neutral between psychological phenomena and objects in the external world. On Russell's account, the components of the world are actual and possible sense-data, not things. Things are constituted out of actual and possible sense-data.

Note that the move to neutral monism seems to be a device to save Russell's view of the meaning of 'being' and 'exists' in conjunction with his extreme empiricism about our talk of objects in the external world. Why should we accept neutral monism? If the reason is merely that it saves Russell's philosophy, then no good reason has been given to accept it. Further, Russell seems to have failed to distinguish between an extremely vivid hallucination and a real object. If Macbeth had hallucinated a dagger being plunged into his arm, felt the pain and hallucinated that blood spurted everywhere, he still would not have seen a real dagger; yet Russell's neutral monism would have been incapable of telling us that there was any difference between Macbeth's particularly vivid and coherent hallucinations and the real world. Even adding other people's perceptions might not help, as they may also experience very similar hallucinations. Of course, Russell might say that such a vivid hallucination is a real physical event, but this would seem to be just a way of saving his view from refutation.

A more important problem is this: the picture natural science gives us of the external world is very different from that given by neutral monism. The objects described by natural science, such as electrons, often have nothing to do with our perceptual faculties. We may be able to perceive some of their properties indirectly by using elaborate instruments. Science shows us objects in the external world often have little to do with how our ordinary perceptual faculties perceive them. Our ordinary perceptual faculties are riddled with distortions, utterly false perceptions and vagueness. For instance, our perception of heat fails to distinguish between conductivity and temperature, and between the preceding state of our bodies and temperature. Water at the same low temperature as air feels colder to us than air because it conducts heat away from us faster than air. When we have been in the heat for some time, cold water will feel much colder than its actual temperature. Thermometers have been designed to overcome such problems. Thermometers have also been designed to give us precise numerical measures rather than vague perceptions of temperature. We have also developed concepts such as specific heat and latent heat to explain what happens in the world, yet we cannot perceive these features of heat but must measure them indirectly. If we were confined to everyday perception, we would be incapable of distinguishing various features of heat in the world. Yet neutral monism tells us that somehow our world is constructed from sense-data.

Russell's account of existence is very strange. It was originally designed to account for our talk about some mathematical truths. As I have said, Russell wanted to interpret the 'is' in sentences like 'there is an even number' as an is of existence. He built this into the formalism which he invented, and which is now standard in much of formal logic. But the view that mathematical objects exist is much more dubious than the view that objects in the external world exist. Objects in the external world have causal interactions with us and with each other. It is far from clear that mathematical objects have any causal powers. In any case, Russell's account as it stands fails to distinguish between mathematical objects and fictional objects. Take the statement that there is only one character called Sherlock Holmes in Conan Doyle's novels. That statement is apparently true of the characters in those novels. Are mathematical truths true in the same kind of way in which truths about objects of fiction are true? Is mathematics a kind of useful fiction? For instance, as the series of natural numbers is now understood, it goes 0, 1, 2, 3 . . . , it is true that zero is the first number in this series. But what is zero? Can the symbol '0' seriously be taken to name an existent object? If it does name an existent object, can it be taken to exist in the same way in which external objects exist? Or is it merely a useful fictional device?

I will not discuss fictional and mathematical objects. It suffices to say here that if these things exist in some sense of 'exist', they do not exist in the same way as objects in the external world.

Fictional objects do not have independent causal powers that allow them to interact with us in a way that is mind independent. In Aristotle's jargon, they are not itselves in terms of themselves. Mathematical objects also do not have causal powers to interact with us, although at least some of them are arguably mind independent in some sense.

It is important to note exactly why Russell's solution is quite inadequate. By talking about propositional functions ranging over objects in the world, Russell has failed to tell us what makes something an object in the external world. On his account, there are unicorns is true if x is a unicorn is true of something in the external world. But he has failed to tell us what it is that makes things part of the furniture of the world so that they can make a statement true. This is the problem Aristotle wanted to solve that Russell has failed to solve. This is what the supposedly obscure talk about being was concerned with.

Despite the problems with Russell's overall view, there is something right about it. Hallucinations are indeed real, but only as representations that seem to be of the external world. They are not part of the world external to our brain, and the external world is not even partly built from them. However, on a modernised Aristotelian account, they too will have an explanation that must ultimately rest on an explanation in terms of the functioning of the brain. But that explanation will have to be provided by the science of the functioning of the brain. Hallucinating a cat will have a scientific explanation of some sort, and it is possible that my hallucinating a cat will be a very specific feature of my brain activity. However, that will be quite different from the real cat.

Another way in which both Russell's and Hume's views are correct is that there is no universal essence that things possess which makes them beings. If Russell's and Hume's view is modified so that 'experience' is understood to be conclusions that are the result of careful experimental work, then they are correct to say that 'experience' does not directly show evidence that the same property is possessed by all beings. To say that being is essence or dependent on essence is not to say that beings all have the same essence. Cats and corundum (ruby and sapphire) do not have the same essence. Neither do individual cats and individual rubies or sapphires. Rather, cats and corundum share a higher-level property of having an essence. This higher-level property is inferred by considering what is necessary to explain general scientific results, such as the periodic table of the elements. This point will be discussed in more detail in chapter 3.

Russell and Hume rightly also raise the problem of how it is that we can have a conception of being without being able to experience it as a separate property. How do we come to have a conception of being?

Ockham's Account of How We Come to Have a Concept of Being

It is hard to find any account of how we come to have the concept of being in Aristotle. The fourteenth-century philosopher William of Ockham offers a very brief empiricist account of how we can acquire the concept of being.

To understand Ockham's explanation of how we acquire a concept of a property of being, we need to start by considering an argument he presents for a property of being, which, following Aristotle, he identified with essence. The argument is much simpler than Aristotle's roundabout refutation of Protagoras and Cratylus. It is this:

> One can prove that there is one common concept predicable of everything in the following way: If there is no one such common then there are different concepts for different things. Let us suppose that there are two such concepts, A and B. Following out this supposition, I can show that some concept more general than A and B is predicable of an object C. Just as we can form the verbal proposition 'C is B', 'C is A', and

'C is something', we can form the three corresponding mental propositions. Two of these are dubious and one is certain; for someone can doubt which of the first two is true, while knowing that the third is true. If this is granted, I argue as follows: The two propositions all have the same subject; therefore, they have different predicates. Were it not so, one and the same proposition would be both certain and dubious; for in the present case the first two are dubious. But if they have different predicates, the predicate in 'C is something' is not the predicate in either 'C is B' or 'C is A'. It is, we can conclude, a different predicate. But it is clear that the relevant predicate is neither less general nor convertible with either A or B. It must therefore be more general. But this is what we set out to prove-that some concept of the mind, different from those that are logically subordinated to it, is common to everything . . . Just as one word is capable of being truly predicated of everything, there is some concept of the mind that can be predicated of every object or of every pronoun referring to an object. (Ockham 1974, 122-3)

Ockham spelled out the same point less abstractly elsewhere when he said:

to the name 'being' there corresponds one common concept that is predicable of all things. I prove this as follows: Let A be 'a human being', let B be 'an animal', and let C be 'Socrates'. Then I argue: Just as one can formulate the three spoken propositions 'C is A', 'C is B', and 'C is a being', so too can one formulate three similar mental propositions, two of which are doubted and the third of which is known. For it is possible that someone should be in doubt with respect to both 'C is A' and 'C is B' and yet know 'C is a being and is something. This is manifestly obvious in the case of something approaching from a distance: When one sees it, he is often in doubt about

> whether it is a human being or an animal or a donkey, and yet he knows evidently that it is a being and is something. Given this, I then argue as follows: Two of these mental propositions are doubtful and the third is known. And the three propositions have exactly the same subject. Therefore, they have distinct predicates. For otherwise the same proposition would at one and the same time be doubtful and certain to the same person – which is impossible; therefore, these three propositions have three distinct predicates. Likewise, it is obvious that the predicate of the third proposition is neither less common than nor interchangeable with any of the other predicates; therefore, it is a predicate that is more common than any of them. (Ockham 1991b, 448–9)

Elsewhere, Ockham makes the same point more simply when he says that

> it sometimes happens, as is evident in the case of something that is approaching me from a distance, that the singular thing causes a sensation by virtue of which I am able to judge only that the thing seen is a being. It is obvious that in such a case the . . . cognition which I have . . . is a cognition of being and not of anything more specific; and consequently, it is neither a specific concept nor a proper concept of a singular thing. (Ockham 1991a, 65)

We do not even have to refer to someone knowing that something is there to accept Ockham's point. It is enough that someone can reasonably believe that something is there in the distance while reasonably leaving open its particular species or genus. We can also expand on his example by considering examples in which it is rational to believe that something causes a phenomenon without yet having a justified belief about the nature of that thing. For instance, radio astronomers can be puzzled about a signal.

Is it a distant pulsar? Pigeon poop on one of their devices? The transmission of a nearby radio station? They can be unsure while being reasonably sure that the signal is caused by something or things, a being or beings.

Ockham clearly shows Hume is wrong to think that the meanings of general terms must be tied to specific types of beings with specific features. We can experience things in a way that is not specific. We can experience them as beings. We can experience other things in a way that shows us that they are caused by something, even though we do not know what it is. We need not accept Ockham's claim that we are sometimes certain of what we see to understand that this is true.

Despite Ockham's argument, it is hard to see how experience alone can give us a conception of an external object. Hume seems to be right in thinking that aspects of our experience do not contain in themselves the idea that they are experiences of external objects, even though Ockham is right that we can experience external objects in a non-specific manner. It is possible for me to mistakenly think that I have seen something through a fog when, in fact, I have imagined it. It is possible for me to hallucinate a cat in the corner of my room that seems to scratch and bite me as I approach it. Even the fact that aspects of my experience are out of my control, such as the apparent scratching and biting, is not enough to give me the idea of an external object. A paranoid delusion might also give me a vivid experience which is out of my conscious control. Where does the idea of a mind independent external object or a mind independent external world come from if not from experience?

A persistent series of experiences of an object, which is confirmed by others, in well-lit circumstances, and in which we can apparently touch and manipulate the object, gives us very good evidence that it exists externally to our minds. However, this does not explain the origins of the idea that there are objects external to our minds.

One plausible suggestion, which comes from Immanuel Kant, is that it is innate in us to think of some of our experiences as being caused by a world external to our minds. We do not have to pursue Kant's complicated argument for this claim to consider it plausible that evolution should have wired into us a tendency to think that some of our experiences are caused by an external world which is independent of our minds. The very idea of an external world which is independent of our minds is an idea that is useful for survival. In any case, although in the previous paragraph I have argued that it is always possible that our most vivid and coherent experiences are hallucinations, and that the objects we think we perceive do not exist, there are various circumstances in which this is very unlikely. Once we have carried out various tests to check whether we are hallucinating or not, we can be pretty sure we are perceiving external objects. I have no space to pursue a discussion of Kant's argument here.

Conclusion

We have seen that Aquinas's, Hume's and Russell's criticisms of the view that being is a property are mistaken. Aquinas is confusing the meaning of terms and the objects referred to by terms. There are also good reasons to reject Russell's account of being. Russell fails to tell us what makes something an inhabitant of the external world as opposed to something which is merely imagined to exist in the external world. However, Russell and Hume are correct to stress that being is not a perceivable property shared by all beings.

Further Readings

I have tried in this chapter to present key segments of the texts of Ockham, Hume and Russell on being. Aquinas's key argument is spelt out in Aquinas, 1937. That work has received some severe criticisms from Anthony Kenny in Kenny, 2002. Russell's theory of existence was anticipated by Gottlob Frege. For a detailed discussion and critique of the Frege/Russell view from an Aristotelian standpoint, see Vikko and Hintikka, 2006. Kant's argument that we bring the assumption of an external world to experience and we do not derive it from experience is presented in his *Refutation of Idealism*, which is part of his *Critique of Pure Reason* (Kant 1996, 288–98; B 274–88). There is a great deal of literature on that argument.

CHAPTER 3

Substance, Essence and Attribute

In his work *Categories*, Aristotle proceeds to categorise kinds of being. He does this by discussing the terms we typically use to describe things. The focus is on distinguishing the metaphysical units of reality, which are in combination in any object. He thinks that these are the kinds of being in the world described at a high level of generality. The terms describing these units can be combined to produce a truth about an object. The truth-maker, the thing that makes the truth true, is a combination of the things described in an object.

It is important to understand that the notion of a truth-maker is not an epistemological notion. Whether some statement is true or not has nothing to do with our knowledge. We may not be able to tell whether some statement is true or not. Nevertheless, if a statement is true, there will be a truth-maker in the world that makes it true. We do not know, and perhaps will never know, whether there are living things in the Andromeda galaxy. Nevertheless, if there are living things there, the statement 'there are living things in the Andromeda galaxy' is true.

While Aristotle lists various kinds of being in *Categories*, I will, in this chapter discuss only three that have been the subject of much debate. They are substance, attribute and individuals.

Chapter 3

Aristotle begins by distinguishing between what is said of a subject, what is in a subject and what is neither in a subject nor said of a subject. The distinction is a little puzzling, but he wants to distinguish between essential properties of the subject (e.g. human, animal) which are said of it, and attributes which are in it (e.g. pale). He also wants to distinguish the individual things which we can name, but which are not said of or in a subject (e.g. Socrates).

Essential properties are properties that a thing cannot lose without becoming something different. If Socrates loses his humanity by dying, he soon turns into a different thing. By contrast, if Socrates loses his paleness in summer, he continues to be Socrates. It is also the case that particular attributes are dependent on the essential properties for their existence, whereas the essential properties are not dependent on the attributes. Socrates must have some attributes, such as a colour, but he does not have to be pale. Further, the attributes are to be explained, in part, by the essential properties. Modernising Aristotle a little, Socrates's genetic inheritance as a caucasian human animal partly explains why he is pale in winter and tanned in summer.

As we have seen in chapter 1, Aristotle indicates that he identifies substance with having an essence. In *Categories* he clearly says that the primary kind of substance is an individual thing with an essence, such as Socrates. However, species which share a common essence are substances in a secondary sense, and the genera to which species belong are substances too. So, humans are a substance in a secondary sense, as are animals. However, in his later work *Metaphysics*, the primary substances seem to be shared essences, such as human. I will put aside in this chapter the discussion of which substances are primary and whether there are shared essences. I will discuss it in the next chapter.

As substance is a key category for Aristotle, it will be necessary to spend some time explaining the connection between substance and essence. Substantia is the term Latin-speaking philosophers invented as a translation of Aristotle's terms ousia (being) and hypokeimenon (underlying thing), which are best understood to be terms describing a primary kind of being. It is not primary in the sense that it is something separate from the being of things. It is primary in the sense that it what explains various features of things and constitutes their identity. It is something we focus on in explanation. It is an aspect of things. Essentia is the term Latin-speaking philosophers invented to translate Aristotle's strange phrase to ti einai (the what it is); that is, what it is that makes something the kind of thing that it is.

Substance and Essence

Aristotle began his metaphysical quest by thinking about a solution to metaphysical problems posed by his predecessor and teacher, Plato. Plato was interested in the question why things in our world come in fairly stable kinds which behave in fairly stable ways. For Plato, it is because things in our world are like the items that he called forms. Forms are unchanging, perfect things which do not exist in our world of changing things. Nevertheless, in some way, things in our world are an imitation of things in the world of forms. For instance, the perfect form of a cat is something cats in our world are like; however, cats in our world do not attain being adult cats until later in their life and then they decay. Instead, the form of cats is eternal and unchanging. Aristotle had the view that talk of mysterious forms in another world was unnecessary and unclear. Instead, taking cats as an example, cats in our world have in them something which makes them grow and develop into cats. This is transmitted from one generation to another generation of cats through sexual reproduction. He thought that this is the form of cats.

To argue for his view about forms, Aristotle had to try to counter the view held by some of his opponents that matter alone is sufficient to explain kinds and things in the world. Aristotle had a detailed view about matter that is not plausible in the light of developments in science. However, parts of his view can be modernised easily. I will focus on those parts of his view. Consider cats yet again. If we were to put all the matter together that composes a cat in a lump, we would not have a cat. The matter must be organised in a particular way so that it functions as a cat. Particular kinds of matter are necessary in order to make a cat; but this is not sufficient to make a cat. For instance, the acids that compose the cat's DNA must be organised into a particular kind of double helix pattern if we are to have a cat that develops from an embryo to a fully grown cat in a typical manner. We may think of the form of the cat as the way some crucial bits of matter in the cat are organised to produce a fully grown cat from the tiniest embryo, and to maintain it once it is fully grown. Whatever that is, is the form of the cat. When it decays or cannot function, the cat dies and becomes a lump of very roughly organised matter.

Aristotle seems to have identified the form of a thing with its essence because he thought that the form, most of all, is responsible for the characteristic powers and capacities of the animal of which it is the essence. Further, while a particular kind of matter is necessary for the essential part of the animal to exist, the matter is constantly changing, whereas the form persists in the animal as long as it exists. We might plausibly disagree with him here and say that the essence of a thing is its formed matter, rather than just its form. Without matter, and a particular kind of matter, a structure cannot exist.

LOCKEAN ESSENCES

Aristotle thought that the paradigmatic things with essences are biological organisms. In the seventeenth century, John Locke turned to considering what gave certain kinds of matter, such as gold, their characteristic powers and liabilities. He believed that the kinds of atoms which composed such things and their arrangement were the source of these powers and liabilities. He thought that the atoms had to be lumps of hard, indivisible matter with little hooks on them. Part of what led him to this belief is the fact that some things could be dissolved in acids but later recovered from acids. For instance, a lump of gold can be dissolved in some acids but stays in them. We know this because, for instance, the same amount of gold can be recovered from the acids. Locke, however, was pessimistic about our ability to discover the essences of things.

Like much of Aristotle's science, Locke's science and his pessimism have been rendered obsolete by later developments. Atoms are not as Locke thought they were, and they are not the ultimate kinds of matter. We have also found out much more through the science of Chemistry than Locke would have thought possible. Nevertheless, it is still plausible to believe that atoms, the arrangement of atoms, and the arrangement inside atoms are the source of the characteristic powers and liabilities of many everyday things, such as lumps of gold. When atoms are broken up, the gold ceases to exist. While the atoms continue to exist, the gold continues to exist. The internal atomic structure of gold can plausibly be identified with the essence of gold. For other things, such as lumps of rusty iron, it is plausible to believe that they are combinations of iron and something else, oxygen. We can see through experiments how rusty iron can be taken apart into iron and oxygen, and then recombined into a lump of rusty iron.

We can leave the details of the science of chemical combinations aside and turn to answering the question: what is the being of the things in we encounter in the everyday world? The modernised Lockean answer is that the being of many of them is atoms or combinations of atoms. The atoms of gold are a unity that explains the characteristic properties of gold. If an individual atom of gold is broken apart into its components, the gold ceases to exist. Note, however, that modernised Lockeans are not claiming that a lump of gold is a unified thing in the sense that an organism is a unified thing. A lump of gold does not have the same unity as an organism. Nevertheless, the reason why the parts of a lump of gold are together and difficult to prise apart is to be found, in part, in the nature of gold. So, the being of the lump as a lump is, in part, to be explained by the nature of gold. (The past history of the lump will be the other part of the explanation of why these parts are together). By contrast, the being of a puddle of water is to be explained, in part, by the chemical combination in its molecular components. The fact that parts of water can be prised apart more easily than the parts of a lump of gold is due to the being of the parts of water. (I leave aside here the difficult task of separating the Hydrogen and Oxygen in water. That is much more demanding because they form a chemical compound.)

Aristotle's Hylomorphism

Readers may have already noticed that we have explanations at two levels in the above discussion. When I was discussing the being of organisms, I suggested that the explanation is to be found in the DNA of organisms and its structure. When we are explaining the being of lumps of a uniform material substance, I suggested the explanation is to be found at the atomic or molecular level. This is similar to a view in Aristotle called hylomorphism, from hyle, the Greek word for matter, and morphe, one of Aristotle's words for form. Hylomorphism holds that what is formed matter at some lower level of explanation is the key part of the matter of a thing at a higher level of explanation in which another form structures the matter. For instance, the acids that form part of the double helix of living organisms are themselves composed of atoms. The hylomorphism can also be pushed downwards in the levels of explanation. Atoms themselves can be pulled part, thereby losing their form; and the protons and electrons which compose them have an essence which constitutes them and explains certain phenomena.

Misleading discussions of Chemistry sometimes make it look as if complex molecules are mere arrangements of atoms, so that all the explaining is done at the atomic level. Models that are used in science classes give the impression that atoms are very much like things with hooks and holes in them that hang together in molecules while retaining their identity. Their form would then be their spatial arrangement. However, this is a simplistic view of things. Molecules are different things from the atoms composing them, and not only in their spatial arrangement. Rather than going into the details of the science, I will use an analogy to explain the point: Think of two light waves of quite different amplitude coming together to make up another light wave which has a different amplitude from either of the preceding light waves. The new light wave is distinct from the preceding light waves. It is not as if the preceding light waves are sitting in it intact, even though they can be got out of it. Take a simple example to illustrate the consequences of this point: water consists of two atoms of Hydrogen and one of oxygen bonded together. However, many of the properties of water are quite distinct from the oxygen and Hydrogen. Oxygen and Hydrogen both burn easily, but water does not burn. This makes much of modern Chemistry more like Aristotle's metaphysical picture of things, in which elements combine to produce something new, rather than Locke's view of Chemistry, in which atoms are treated as bits of solid matter with hooks and holes in them.

It is unclear how far Aristotle's picture of the world, in which formed matter from a lower level can be integrated as matter to produce formed matter at a higher level of explanation, can be plausibly applied. For instance, is the matter of ecosystems whole organisms? Is the matter of human societies individual human beings? I will leave these interesting questions aside. It suffices for our purposes to stress that, on the Aristotelian picture I am trying to defend, the formed matter of things at some different levels will be importantly different, and hence their being will be importantly different.

What Are Essences?

So far, I have talked only a little about what essences might be. Of course, modern science needs to discover the essences of things; but Metaphysics should be able to give us some contours of the nature of essences. On Aristotle's account, essences are to be identified with the characteristic capacities or powers and liabilities, of formed matter.

This is an account which is meant to be compatible with hylomorphism. For instance, on a modernised Aristotelianism, the essence of gold is not just its characteristic atomic structure. Rather, the atomic structure is understood to be identical to its characteristic powers and liabilities. It is the kind of thing it is. This ties into one modern account of essences, which is that they are themselves powers (and liabilities), spatiotemporally located and having a spatial form.

Let us discuss chemical and also mineralogical kinds further. The characteristic powers and liabilities of these kinds are invariant, with the exception of isotopes of these kinds. (Isotopes of a chemical element vary in the number of neutrons in their nucleus. Their chemical properties are the same as the element, but they differ in some of their physical properties. For instance, so-called heavy water, which contains an isotope of Hydrogen called deuterium, can be used as a coolant in certain kinds of nuclear reactors, whereas ordinary water cannot be used in that way.) If we were to classify by isotope, their powers and liabilities would be invariant. Here, we can perhaps think of the essence of an isotope as the essence of a kind, rather than the essence of an individual.

BIOLOGICAL INDIVIDUALS

What is the essence of a human individual, such as a woman? The essence of a human being might be thought to be its characteristic capacities, such as its rationality, as well as the capacities it shares with many other animals. This is presumably why medieval philosophers striving to give a real definition of human beings suggested that the definition is rational animal. (A real definition is a definition which describes the essence of a thing correctly.) However, we can easily see that rational animal as a real definition is inadequate. For a start, very young infants are not capable of many tasks that adults can perform. We would need to understand our definition as stating a capacity that human beings can develop over time, rather than something they have at the outset. There is the further problem that human beings vary in their abilities. Some humans with intellectual or physical disabilities cannot develop some of these powers, even over time. We can try to argue that we are talking about normal as opposed to abnormal human beings, but this seems arbitrary. In any case, modern Biology has taught us that there is a great deal of variation among members of a species, particularly in a species that has a wide geographical distribution. Male and female members of many species often differ in their powers as well. Many females can give birth, for instance; males cannot.

To deal with the problems in the last paragraph, it might be thought that it is better to think of essences of individual organisms. Aristotle's primary examples of such things in *Categories* are biological individuals, which he thinks are substances. We have already seen that things other than biological individuals can have essences, for instance, lumps of minerals or lumps of chemical elements. Yet it should be emphasised that there is an important sense in which these things are different from biological individuals. Biological individuals have an essence which makes them unified things whose parts function together to promote survival and reproduction. Although they shed parts over time and gain other parts, they cannot lose many parts at a single time and survive. They also grow over time and, later, decay over time. This functional unity and trajectory of growth and decay over time is the result of a long evolutionary history. As Aristotle recognised, biological individuals are best understood diachronically. Earlier stages of embryonic development function so that they can develop into an adult individual capable of surviving and reproducing. This is why some philosophers have thought that biological individuals are best understood as processes located in space over time, rather than things.

Chapter 3

To understand the force of Aristotle's view that biological organisms are paradigmatic individuals, contrast a human being with a lump of gold. The lump of gold can be broken up into bits, while the bits continue to be gold. The gold does not have functional parts and does not have a trajectory of development. Some lumps of minerals are in crystalline structures that are difficult to break apart into separate parts that are themselves the same mineral. There is a kind of natural unity in these lumps, but it is not the natural unity of a biological organism. Still, minerals and elements can be broken up into other things with some difficulty, and only by using techniques that affect them at very tiny levels. To break up minerals, we need to break up the molecules that constitute them. Breaking up elements is more difficult, for we need to descend to below the level of the atom. So, there is a sense in which very tiny parts of minerals and elements are individuals with a natural unity.

Even so, as I have noted, biological organisms have a trajectory of growth and decay. The capacities of adults are different from those of children. We have encountered an important problem not sufficiently recognised by earlier Aristotelians. To explain the patterns of growth and decay of individual organisms, and their changes in capacities over time, we have to revert to something more basic, such as active DNA (DNA can continue to exist inactive in dead organisms, even though it does not perform its function). However, as I have noted in chapter 1, deciding questions about essences is best left in the end to natural science.

It is important to note here that we explain different things when we explain the characteristic powers and capacities of human beings as opposed to treating human beings as already having capacities or powers. A biological account explains how it is that human beings come to develop capacities or powers in terms of underlying powers and capacities, such as those of active DNA. Another sort of account takes the capacities and powers of a flourishing human being for granted and seeks to explain what they do. It was such an account that the medievals were attempting when they used rational animal as a definition of human beings.

CRITICISMS OF SUBSTANCE AND ESSENCE

Philosophers in the empiricist tradition have been wary of both the notion of substance and the notion of essence. Some of their wariness originates in a naïve empiricist view of the origin of concepts. As I said in the introduction, I will ignore such views here, as they have been replaced by much more sophisticated views in cognitive science. Some of their wariness, however, originates in scepticism about our ability to comprehend the hidden structure of the world. Other origins of their scepticism originate in a concentration on Physics as a science.

I will only reply briefly here to these sorts of scepticism here. Biology and medicine are well-developed sciences. To do experiments in Biology and medicine, we need to identify and later re-identify particular organisms. We also need to identify the mechanisms responsible for their growth and development and observe how these mechanisms act at a later time. All of this requires that we treat organisms as re-identifiable particulars with a history in which their attributes change over time. Aristotle's substance/attribute Metaphysics was not developed only to deal with abstract problems; it was developed also, and perhaps primarily, to deal with real problems in Biology. It is well known that Aristotle was an important pioneer in Biology and wrote a great deal about the subject. While Physics is a more fundamental science, it does not replace the insights of Biology, nor does it make the picture of the world that is required for Biology to be a science redundant.

Let me turn now to Chemistry and Mineralogy. Chemistry and Mineralogy are organised by identifiable kinds, which focus on the capacities/powers of natural kinds that have been discovered by rigorous scientific experiments on re-identifiable individual instances that belong to the kinds. Again, while Physics is more fundamental, that does not make Chemistry or Mineralogy redundant, nor does it make the picture of the world required for those sciences false.

ATTRIBUTES AND DISPOSITIONS

Aristotle gives a perhaps confused account of attributes in *Categories*. He gives a much fuller account of attributes in the *Metaphysics*. In that work, attributes are a secondary kind of being, dependent for their existence on the substances in which they inhere. Among attributes, there are features like colour, which can be further subdivided into particular colours. Things and features of things come in particular qualities at particular times. For instance, Socrates is very pale in winter, less pale in spring and much less pale in summer. The quantities of the same thing, which are also attributes, can change over time as well. Children are very small when they are young and are bigger when they are grown up.

An important question that arises is whether some or all attributes are really just dispositions. For example, while Aristotle seems to have thought that colour properties are intrinsic properties which are revealed by light, by the time of Locke, research indicated that coloured light is caused by the reflection of aspects or parts of white light off surfaces. The surfaces are disposed to reflect various kinds of light but not others. Further, the perception of colour is caused by a disposition of perceivers to perceive various kinds of light by modifying them in various ways. For instance, we now know human perceivers perceive particular colours as fairly constant over surfaces – this is a product of the brain's interaction with the wavelengths of light, and not just of the wavelengths of light. Perceiving more complex differences in wavelength would overload our brains with information that is not useful to our survival. Our brain is also primarily sensitive to relations between wavelengths of light rather than to the intrinsic properties of wavelengths of light, presumably because this is what counted in the ancestral environment in which we evolved. Our sensitivity to relations between wavelengths of light is something that has been known to painters for a long time. The colours in a painting will look realistic if it preserves relations between colours, even if the individual colours in the painting are different from the colours in reality. The British painter John Constable studied these properties and exploited them in the nineteenth century without having a satisfactory empirical theory of how they work. In addition, we perceive colour as if it were intrinsic to surfaces rather than to the light reflected off them, which is why Aristotle made the mistake of thinking colour is intrinsic to surfaces.

Colours are properties we are disposed to perceive as properties of the surfaces we perceive. This seems to be a result of a long evolutionary history in which the dispositional properties of objects to primarily reflect certain wavelengths of light when surrounded by other objects in an ancestral environment were important to our survival. This is why we naturally project the colour onto certain objects themselves. This is what makes the 'illusions' produced by skilled painters possible. It was not the wavelengths of light themselves which were important to our survival. So, we see in the case of perceived colour that it is the result of the disposition of surfaces to reflect certain sorts of light as well as the disposition of perceivers to respond in particular ways to the light. Whether we want to say that colour is really there or not on the basis of these facts is a trivial semantic problem. Colour is not there independently of a particular kind of perceiver with a particular evolutionary history. Objects in themselves have no colour.

Dispositions are just powers or capacities. How far can we take this account of attributes? Is it the case that all attributes are really powers? Take shape, for example. Is the shape of an object just a power? No doubt the shape of an object can have an effect because a spherical object, for instance, can roll, whereas a square object cannot. No doubt a spherical object has the power to roll in virtue of its sphericity, but it is hard to see that its shape alone gives it the power to roll. Nevertheless, this is true of many features of objects. A massive object only has the power to fall down in a gravitational field. Socrates's skin only has the power to turn brown in ultraviolet light. Powers only can have effects when interacting with other things of particular kinds. So perhaps the shape of an object is a power after all – but is it nothing but a power? It seems that the shape of an object exists independently of its powers – it is a spatial feature which exists independently of a capacity to do something. This makes it distinct from things like the power of Socrates's skin. Some philosophers claim that shape is a feature which is a categorical property and not, or not merely, a dispositional property. Indeed, some philosophers seek to explain powers by underlying categorical properties. I will discuss the important distinction between dispositional and categorical properties in the next chapter. Before I turn to that chapter, let me emphasise something. Attributes are not some free-floating items that happen to ride on substances. They are aspects of things, or of the interaction of things with other things, on which we can focus our attention.

Conclusion

We have seen that Aristotle's distinction between substance and attribute is important in various sciences, particularly in Biology. We have also seen that Aristotle's claim that substance is essence is a plausible claim. In addition, modified Lockean additions to Aristotle's view allow us to extend his essentialism to chemical kinds and isotopes. Finally, we have seen that attributes are a secondary kind of being, dependent on substances for their existence. As well, in our exploration of the nature of attributes, we have briefly discussed the view that some or all attributes are really powers in substances, which will be discussed further in the next chapter.

FURTHER READINGS

Aristotle's discussion of substance in *Categories* is Aristotle 1963, 5–12; 2a11-4b19. His account of attributes in *Categories* (sometimes translated as qualities) is found in Aristotle 1963, 24–31; 8b25-11a39. The book by Vasilis Politis I listed in further readings contains an excellent account of Aristotle's use of these concepts in *Categories* and *Metaphysics*. Politis plausibly calls substance 'primary being' and attribute 'non-primary being'. John Locke's *An Essay Concerning Human Understanding*, Book II, chapter XXIII, sections 1–29, which is available in various editions, contains an important discussion of substance and power. However, it is marred by mixing up an empiricist epistemology with Metaphysics. A useful account of Locke on substance that starts with Aristotle is presented in Lowe 1995, 67–93. An important but rather abstract argument for re-identifiable particulars as basic in our conceptual scheme is presented in Strawson 1959. Strawson was influenced by Aristotle and Kant and interpreted Aristotle in the light of Kant. As will be obvious, I think it is Aristotle's scientific investigations that were crucial. The insights and failures of Aristotle's Biology are discussed in detail by a distinguished developmental biologist in Le Roi 2014.

A very different account of material objects, which holds that they are just compresent properties (properties that exist at the same place and at the same time), is presented by so-called 'trope' theorists. A good account of trope theories is given in the *Stanford Encyclopedia of Philosophy* online.

Chapter 4

Universals, Particulars and Dispositions

A striking feature of the world is that things resemble one another in certain respects, and that their behaviour is predictable under ideal conditions by paying close attention to these respects. The laws of Physics, for instance, deal with properties like mass, and they apparently describe numerical relations between the mass of things and other properties. By knowing the mass of an object, we can, under ideal conditions, work out how fast it will fall when it is in a position in the gravitational field of a planet or a moon. We can also calculate how powerful its impact will be on its surface, and what forces are required to resist its gravitational forces. This is what allowed us to send people to the surface of the moon and return them to earth. Consider how remarkable are these features of our world. While modern science has greatly refined our knowledge of the world, classifying things and their properties is a feature of human thought without which we would be unable to survive. If things did not come in at least rough kinds, we would be unable to gain knowledge about those kinds and communicate that knowledge to others by using general terms.

Through his biological studies, Aristotle made or collected some crucial observations about different kinds of animals. These included observations about the ways in which different kinds of animals survive and reproduce, speculations and observations about why certain parts of them are useful for their way of life, and so on. The very fact that animals come in kinds is something that struck Aristotle as a key feature of the world. He classified them into species and genera in a way that anticipates recent developments.

We have seen in the last chapter that Aristotle thought of the world as consisting of individual things which have an essence. Socrates is essentially human, for instance. Aristotle attributed an important explanatory role to essences. For example, he thought that what distinguishes the capacities and characteristic activities of Plato, Socrates, Aristotle and so on from other animals and from other things is their humanity. Plato had tried to explain such commonalities by postulating an immaterial form of humanity which somehow influences things in our world. Aristotle rejected Plato's account because it postulates mysterious entities, and because there was no clear account of how such entities could influence things in our world. In *Categories* Aristotle thought that individual things are the primary substances, whereas in *Metaphysics* it seems that shared essences are the primary substances. Arguably, different accounts of explanation are involved in Aristotle's two views. If individual things are the primary substances, then what explains the capacity of an individual thing is its essence which happens to be very similar to the essence of certain other things – this is what makes them the same kind of thing. There are no forms or anything of the kind. Species are only secondary substances in an attenuated sense of 'substance'. By contrast, if shared essences are the primary substances, then the kinds explain the similarity of capacities of individual things. Unlike Plato, Aristotle seems to have thought of the universal shared essence as something in this world which is inherent in all instances of humans. On Aristotle's view, if there were no humans, there would be no universal essence of humanity.

Aristotle knew that there were deviant members of biological kinds. He thought of nature as producing a result for the most part. He also sometimes thought that deviant members of a kind were monsters of some sort. Since Darwin and the genetic revolution, biological thought has led us to understand that species are often rubbery sorts of things. Over a large geographical area, there can be great variation in the capacities of members of a species who can nevertheless interbreed. Over time, species also change gradually or relatively suddenly into other species. So, Aristotle's view of shared essences is no longer plausible. However, some philosophers think that shared properties provide a good explanation at a more fundamental level, for instance at the level of electrons. This view has been most vigorously defended by David Armstrong in recent times. Armstrong thinks of the fundamental things in the world as sharing certain universal properties. On his account, scientific laws capture the relations between universals. A thing consists of particular features such as its location in space and time, and universals which it shares with other things of the same kind. Armstrong's view is a revival of the view Aristotle seems to defend in *Metaphysics* added to the discoveries of modern science.

A rival view, often called 'nominalism', holds that everything in the world is a particular. Universals do not exist. It is called 'nominalism' because it holds that it is the name we give to things that exactly resemble other things in certain respects is what they have in common. For instance, the things we call 'masses' all have an individual mass. They do not share a universal. This view was defended in the Middle Ages by Ockham; it became the standard view in the scientific revolution and in early modern philosophy. Descartes, Locke, and many others, held that only particulars exist. Nominalism attracted many empiricist philosophers. If we look in the world, no matter how refined our scientific techniques, all we seem to observe are particulars, and spatial and temporal relations between particulars. Experiments to determine the causal powers of things are all done on particulars. This is a strong prima facie argument for the claim that universals do not exist.

I will only discuss one popular variety of nominalism, resemblance nominalism. Resemblance nominalism holds that individual things resemble one another in a variety of ways, and sometimes the resemblance is an exact resemblance. Take spherical things. Balls, planets, stars, and many other things resemble one another in being nearly spherical. Perhaps there are even things that are exactly spherical, although I know of none. The behaviour of approximately spherical things in various contexts is predictable to a high degree by taking account of their approximate sphericality plus other key features and applying the laws of Physics. The resemblance nominalist will stress that they are nevertheless importantly different from one another in the degree to which they approximate a geometrically ideal sphericality. She will stress that, at least in most cases, sphericality is an idealisation.

Arguments for the Existence of Universals

The first argument is that we need to appeal to universals to talk coherently about resemblances. Suppose we pursue a nominalist strategy and say that things resemble one another in various respects. What are the respects in which things resemble one another? They are certain properties, such as mass. We need to distinguish such properties from other properties of things. How do we do this? By referring to a property. However, if a property is not a universal, it is argued that it is mysterious how we are able to distinguish such properties.

A second related argument is that if we assume the existence of universals, we have a simple explanation for exact resemblance. It is that there is a shared universal between all the things that exactly resemble one another.

A third argument is due to Bertrand Russell. It is that

> *[I]f we wish to avoid the universals whiteness and triangularity, we shall choose some particular patch of white or some particular triangle, and say that anything is white or*

a triangle if it has the right sort of resemblance to our chosen particular. But then the resemblance required will have to be a universal. Since there are many white things, the resemblance must hold between many pairs of particular white things; and this is characteristic of a universal. It will be useless to say that there is a different resemblance for each pair, for then we will have to say that these resemblances resemble each other, and thus at last we shall be forced to admit resemblance as a universal. (Russell 1997, 96)

A fourth, and perhaps most important, argument is that if things are merely particulars, it is mysterious why things which apparently share a property, such as mass, behave in a manner which can be put as a law of nature. By contrast, assuming that things are particulars which have genuine universal properties explains easily why things which share those properties have a law-like relation to things which share other properties. Postulating universals as the source of law-likeness would solve two problems at once: it would explain the existence of natural laws; and it would explain why observing a limited sample of things of a kind allows us to extrapolate to a universal – that is to say, it would solve Hume's famous puzzle about why induction from particulars to a universal is often successful, even though such an inference is deductively invalid.

SOME RESPONSES TO ARGUMENTS FOR UNIVERSALS

The first argument for universals is not convincing. Our everyday perception and measurement instruments allow us to distinguish various properties of particular things. When we see and pick up a thing, we see that it has various properties we can distinguish. We can distinguish its sphericality from its weight, for instance. We can pick a group of paradigmatic examples of particular properties and judge the resemblance of another instance to those properties. That is how standards of mass were initially decided, even though the paradigmatic example of a kilogram varied by a tiny amount over time. We can also idealise certain properties in our minds. Seeing a cricket ball and a tennis ball resemble one another in sphericality, we can construct an idealised sphericality even if we know of nothing which is exactly spherical.

The second argument for universals is one of the most powerful. It seems to offer a simple explanation of exact resemblance. However, it runs against everyday observation. Suppose we pick up two objects in succession weighing exactly 1 kilogram. They are located in different places. We do not observe anything universal – we only observe that the two different objects show the same weight on our scales. This does not rule out an explanation in terms of universals, but it makes it more problematic. Unless we need universals in our explanation, there is no need to postulate them. I will discuss whether we need universals in the next section.

The third argument for universals deserves a more careful reply. The reply is that there are internal relations, and resemblances are internal relations. By an internal relation, I do not mean anything mysterious. Take two things which have a similar mass, for instance, two cats, Binky and Twinky. Their similarity does not consist of an additional thing, the relation between them – Russell is right in thinking that that would lead to a regress. Rather, Binky and Twinky are similar just in virtue of the mass of each cat. This solution can be applied to the resemblance between various things. We do not need resemblances between pairs of things which then resemble relations between other pairs of things. Many things can just resemble one another in some respect without the need for an external thing, the relation between them.

I will criticise the fourth argument for universals in a later section.

Categorical and Dispositional Properties

To spell out my criticisms of the existence of universals, I will first need to discuss categorical and dispositional properties. The distinction between categorical and dispositional properties has its roots in Aristotle and in his predecessor, Plato. Let us start with dispositions. The Greeks used Greek words which roughly correspond to the English words power or capacity. We will call powers, capacities and the like dispositions, as they are words to describe the dispositions things have to do things either to themselves or to interact with other things. A human child is disposed to convert food it eats into parts of itself. A glass is disposed to be fragile.

Aristotle thought that, due to their essence, individual things had the disposition to become something. He was thinking primarily of biological organisms, which have the capacity or power to become adult organisms of a particular kind that reproduce themselves. Nevertheless, he sometimes used the notion of a disposition to explain other kinds of behaviour of things in the world. The details need not detain us here. We have seen how Locke used the notion of a power to explain our colour perceptions. Many things have dispositions to interact with other things in various ways. Going back to an example I used in the last chapter, Socrates's skin has the disposition to turn brown when exposed to ultraviolet light. We can give many other examples. Magnets have the disposition to attract iron, large moving objects have the disposition to move small objects with which they collide, and so on.

It is important to grasp that dispositions do not invariably produce the results they are disposed to produce. Glass that is wrapped in bubble wrap will not break when it is dropped on a hard floor. A disposition can be countered by another disposition. Further, in describing dispositions, we describe only some aspects of a thing. The disposition of a piece of iron in a strong magnetic field and its disposition in a strong gravitational field are both aspects of it. They can interact to produce an effect in the iron that is different from both of its dispositions.

Chapter 4

When we turn to categorical properties, these are more difficult to explain. It is sometimes said that categorical properties are attributes or qualities, but this is misleading. Some categorical features are certainly attributes or qualities. Socrates's colour is one of these. However, when recent philosophers talk of categorical properties, they are often thinking of features like the molecular structure of something. Take water as an example, whose structure is H_2O; that is to say that in water, two atoms of Hydrogen are in a bond with one atom of oxygen. According to this view, the molecule is of a certain size and shape and has various other features independently of its dispositional properties. The relations between universals in laws of nature explain what happens. On Armstrong's view, the relations between universals are contingent, and not necessary. The laws of nature are facts, but contingent facts. The world could have been radically otherwise, as we can imagine if we think of counterfactual possibilities. By contrast, Brian Ellis has argued that things have both categorical and dispositional properties. According to him, the laws of nature are dispositional. They are natural necessities.

It is difficult to see how the laws of nature can be just contingent. If they were, things would exist without having any essence at all. It is hard to see how a cat or a molecule could exist without having an intrinsic essence that makes it behave in a particular way under certain conditions. What, for example, would make something a cat if it did not have characteristic dispositional properties? What would distinguish it from a hallucination? Charles Martin and John Heil have argued in some detail that dividing off categorical and dispositional properties is a mistake, and that the categorical and dispositional properties of things are identical. For instance, the dispositions or powers of a molecule of H_2O are its dispositional properties, and they are also its categorical properties. So, according to them, there is no gain in explanatory power in invoking categorical properties.

We can understand the Martin/Heil view better if we consider what makes water molecules behave as they do. Water molecules are disposed to cohere in a jumbled state, which is what produces surface tension in water. Try pushing down on water and you will feel the resistance. This is both a dispositional and a categorical property of the water molecules jumbled together. When the water is very cold, the molecules form a crystalline structure, which is both a dispositional and categorical property which we call ice.

Martin and Heil can explain a great deal. However, the spatial arrangement and the spatial position of molecules are to some extent independent of the causal powers of the molecules. The position and shape of a molecule, like everything else, are affected by the causal powers of space and by surrounding materials. In a very curved space, a molecule's geometry will be different. The molecule will in turn have an influence on space, although a very small one. The causal powers of space will be discussed further in the chapter on space. The causal powers of things are affected by the external relations into which they enter. Relations will be discussed in the chapter on relations.

Natures and Laws of Nature

Having explained the Martin/Heil view and its limitations, I want to turn to the so-called laws of nature. In the eighteenth century, David Hume, like his contemporaries, wanted to reject what he thought were the bogus explanations involved in many scholastic discussions influenced by Aristotle. He denied that we have any knowledge of the powers (dispositions) underlying what happens in the world. He declared them to be mysterious. Instead, he proposed that we observe regularities and generalise from a few instances of those regularities. This involved him in a conundrum. He was unable to justify a generalisation from what happens in a few instances to what happens as a universal law – yet apparently, various scientists , such as Isaac Newton, had recently produced just such universal laws. In the twentieth century, Hume's successors produced elaborate accounts of inductive generalisation to deal with this problem.

Hume also had great trouble justifying our belief in the existence of material things, as he denied that we have any knowledge of essences or dispositions. He failed to give any plausible account of how a vivid hallucination is different from a real thing, as I pointed out in chapter 2. In the early twentieth century, Bertrand Russell and the logical positivists, who wanted to have all our knowledge of the world ultimately based on what we get through direct experience, used various devices to get around this problem. I have discussed the inadequacies of those devices in Russell's work in chapter 2. The devices involving various formal and linguistic strategies became more elaborate as time went on.

One problem with the Humean account is that it presented experience as if it were a group of theory-neutral sensations. However, this does not adequately describe our experience. We feel things pushing against us and pressing down on us. Pick up a suitcase with a high mass and you will feel a strong pull downwards. Experience is riddled with experiences of powers and forces. These 'theories' are built into experience for evolutionary reasons. We do not have experiences without experiencing them as something, for instance, something pushing on us or pulling on us. Again, we do not experience a series of sensations when we see a material object. We see it as a material object. Our experience is of an object in space because our brain uses images from two eyes or scans from one eye to produce a representation of a material object. Further, turn your head from side to side. You do not just experience changing sensations. You experience your head changing position while your body remains in a fixed place. In short, experience comes with what might be called 'natural interpretations' wired into us.

While various philosophers were producing elaborate stories based on an empiricist theory of knowledge, science was producing knowledge through experiments to discover the dispositions of things and the strength of those dispositions. The experiments involved elaborate methods for blocking off or minimising the strength of other dispositions. A completely different picture was emerging of how the world works to the picture that Hume had proposed.

In addition, many of the so-called laws that were being produced were ceteris paribus (all other things being equal), that is, they dealt with situations in which other factors were not interfering. They described the dispositions of things, such as the forces they exert in various situations. Other laws dealt with idealised objects, such as ideal gases, which consist of point particles that do not interact electrically. These sorts of moves had already been prefigured by Aristotle.

First, Aristotle clearly realised that the science of his day was only able to describe things that happened for the most part under certain conditions. He knew, for instance, about biological abnormalities, though he did not know the causes of many of those abnormalities. Of course, he had not invented experimental science, in which we work out conditions under which only certain factors are germane to the outcome. While some experimental science occurred in antiquity, it was not practised in the highly systematic way which has become much more common since the seventeenth century.

Second, consider Aristotle's account of how we construct the science of geometry. Aristotle had argued that geometry works by abstraction, by which he meant not that it deals with strange abstract objects, but that we leave out various features of objects in geometrical work and concentrate only on certain features. When dealing with a square table, we deal only with its ends; we treat them as lines which have no thickness, points which have no size, and so on. Yet these are not objects of our experience. We get them by focussing only on certain features of our experience. Aristotle also knew that we idealise objects, though he presented no systematic account of that phenomenon – experience does not present us with perfectly round spheres or perfectly flat surfaces. These are the products of both abstraction and idealisation.

Abstraction and idealisation abound in science. They are the only ways we know in which we can deal with a very complex world. However, as Nancy Cartwright has emphasised, objects in the world do not come that way. When we separate out the electrical forces in gases from their mechanical behaviour, we are telling a kind of useful lie. In the world, an atom or a molecule has both dispositions at the same time. Further, there are no things which are ideal gases, which are treated as points with mechanical properties in science. This, too, is a lie. Causes are real as dispositions of things. However, laws of nature in Physics are useful lies.

This means that the fourth argument for universals from laws of nature can also be rebutted. The fundamental laws of nature are either ceteris paribus laws, which apply only if counteracting factors are not at work, or they are universal. If they are universal, they deal with the dispositions of things and are only a partial description of things. What we observe in the world is usually the result of various dispositions interacting. For instance, the gravity of the earth disposes a train to be on rails on the ground. However, a maglev train uses powerful magnets to create a resisting force to keep a train off the ground. What we see in the world is not explained by relations between universals, for the laws do not tell us what things will do, but only what they are disposed to do. In a particular situation where a resisting force occurs, a thing will behave quite differently from a situation in which there is no resisting force.

ARGUMENTS AGAINST THE EXISTENCE OF UNIVERSALS

On Armstrong's and related views, relations between universals are supposed to explain what things do in certain circumstances. This brings us to the first argument against universals. Take some salt dissolving in water. Many other instances of salt are not dissolving in water. If the relations between universals account were true, we would expect all the instances of salt to be dissolving in water. However, they are not. The instances of the water and salt need to be brought together in order for the salt to dissolve in water. A simple explanation would appeal to the nature of the instance of salt which is dissolving. There is no need to appeal to an underlying universal. One way to try to fix this problem is to argue that there is both the essence of the instance of salt and the universal. The essence of the instance of salt explains why it is dissolving; the universal explains the law-like relation between salt and dissolving. However, this leads to the problem of explaining how the universal causes the activity of the instance. Aristotle seems to have intended to get around the problem of how one of Plato's forms could cause something in our world by postulating immanent universals. Nevertheless, a very similar problem now seems to arise to the problem raised by Plato's forms. How does the universal interact with the essence of the instance? A causal process of some kind must be invoked if we are to make sense of such an interaction. However, we have no idea what this process could be.

A second, related argument is that it is entirely unclear how a universal acts, even if we put aside the problem in the previous paragraph. We see or detect particulars acting. As we have seen, particulars cause. It is unclear how universals can affect one another to form laws. Armstrong thinks of laws as contingent relations among universals. Brian Ellis seems to think of them as necessary relations. We are never told how exactly the universals connect with one another in the relevant way. A mysterious method of action seems to be being postulated. If we do not need to add mysterious methods of action to our explanations, we should dispense with them.

A third argument is that postulating a universal is an unnecessary multiplication of entities. First, we need to postulate universals as well as particulars to explain the behaviour of things even though we do not observe universals but only instances. Second, it is unclear where we should stop in this process of postulating entities. A mass of one kilogram and a mass of two kilograms behave differently in many situations. They do not exactly resemble one another in mass. This is disguised in statements of laws like Newton's Second Law, Force Equals Mass Times Acceleration, which state general mathematical relations between particular aspects of things. If we follow the account of defenders of universals, why should we not postulate a universal of one kilogram mass and a universal of two-kilogram mass? That could be a universal which is immanent in those masses. By contrast, Newton's Second Law cannot be immanent in those individual masses as it describes a general mathematical relation. If we postulate a universal for masses of every size, we will need to postulate an enormous, possibly infinite, number of universals, for masses vary slightly in their mass.

What about objects that resemble one another but do not share exactly the same property? Take almost spherical objects such as balls. They resemble one another in being almost spherical, but they differ slightly in how much they approach being spherical. Do we need to postulate a different universal for each ball type? However, if we say that the universal is simply sphericity, we have failed to take account of important differences between the behaviour of a ball that is more nearly spherical than another ball. Do we need an infinite number of universals of almost spherical things? In such cases, it is much simpler to treat sphericity and similar properties as idealisations, which are useful for calculational purposes.

Conclusion

We have seen that the view that law-likeness in the world is to be explained by the existence of universals is implausible in a variety of ways. We have also seen that scientific laws are either ceteris paribus laws or describe dispositions that can be countered by other dispositions. They are not contingent relations between universals, for they do not describe the universal behaviour of things. In any case, particular laws do not exhaustively describe the dispositions of things. A law that describes the mechanical properties of things is an abstraction from its various properties, such as its electromagnetic and chemical properties, which may be crucial in certain situations. In addition, much of Physics uses idealised properties which do not or might not exist in the world – properties like sphericity might not exist in the world but are useful for predicting the behaviour of things which are approximately spherical in certain circumstances.

Further Readings

Various views about Aristotle on universals in *Categories* and *Metaphysics* are very clearly explained in Loux (2013). Politis (2004) argues that Aristotle is not committed to the existence of immanent universals in any of his work.

The view that relations between universals explain the existence of laws has been ably put and defended by David Armstrong in Armstrong (1989), which also contains a luminous account of the debate about universals and of the various philosophical positions about universals. Martin and Heil explain their dispositional view and critique of universals in Martin and Heil 1999. An important critique of universals and defence of the dispositional account is Heil (2003). Brian Ellis tries to marry aspects of both positions in Ellis (2001).

Nancy Cartwright discusses the relation between the Aristotelian view about powers and modern science in Cartwright (1999). Her critique of universal laws of nature is Cartwright (1983). Her defence of powers, which she calls capacities, is Cartwright (1989). Some of Cartwright's arguments rely on a thorough knowledge of Physics.

CHAPTER 5

Relations

Among his *Categories*, Aristotle lists the category of relation (Aristotle 1963, 17–24; 6a36-8b24). Aristotle is primarily thinking of the relations between two or more substantial individuals; for instance, Socrates is of the same species as Plato. He treats relations that individuals enter into as properties of the individuals at a time. The relation between them is not a separate thing. It is merely the fact that Socrates is human and Plato is human. This point is made very clearly in an argument in his *Metaphysics*. Aristotle says that

> *relatives least of all are entities or real objects . . . relatives alone do not come into being or pass away or change in the way that increase and diminution occur in quantity, alteration in quality, locomotion in place, sheer coming to be and passing away in the case of a real object. There is none of this with relatives.* (Aristotle 1976, 118; 1088a 23–34)

Aristotle treats even relations in which something seems to be directed at another thing as properties of the thing in question, and not as a separate thing. For instance, he would have treated Abelard loves Eloise as a property of Abelard somehow directed towards Eloise. However, note that change of place is real for

Aristotle because he thinks place is real. I will discuss what he means by his remarks on space in the next chapter.

What is driving Aristotle? Why doesn't he just admit the existence of relations as additional beings external to individuals? We can only speculate, as Aristotle is not explicit on the matter. However, a plausible speculation is that Aristotle's empiricism is driving his reluctance to admit such entities. After all, while we can clearly see a human and her changing attributes, a relation seems to be a strange thing which we cannot directly perceive.

Criticisms of the Aristotelian View

Aristotle's argument in *Metaphysics* is problematic. There is an important sense in which some relations do pass away. Spatial relations are an example. If I move the things on my table further apart from one another, then the distance relation between them has passed away. We can add to this that the gravitational force between objects changes by changing their spatial distance. Nevertheless, Aristotle seems to have exempted change of place from his view, as I noted above. So, this is not so much a problem for Aristotle as it is for some of his recent followers.

In modern times, Bertrand Russell and other philosophers have argued that Aristotle's view of relations is fundamentally mistaken. In their view, relations are external to the individuals involved in the relation. They are existing things that individuals enter into or produce, while continuing to be those individuals. Hence, a substance-attribute ontology that denies the existence of external relations is insufficient for grasping the nature of the world.

Russell was one of the major innovators in logic who made Aristotle's syllogistic logic obsolete. Aristotle's logic can handle inferences involving statements like 'All men are mortal' and 'Socrates is a man'. However, it is not adequate for dealing with inferences involving statements like 'Everyone loves someone' or 'the number 3 is next in the series of natural numbers after

2'. The inadequacies of Aristotelian logic are particularly clear when dealing with inferences that deal with mathematical truths or truths of Physics. Russell's claims about the inadequacies of Aristotelian logic are accepted by logicians, so I will not go into the details of modern logic here. Russell thought that the inadequacies of Aristotelian logic arise from the fact that Aristotle wrongly denied that relations are external to the objects involved in the relations.

In his critique of those who deny the existence of external relations, Russell was particularly focussed on order relations. Take a series of weights arranged in a line, starting from the lightest weight and going on to the heaviest weight. Each weight is heavier than its predecessor. Now, it seems clear that here we have not only the intrinsic properties of each weight, but something else. Starting from the lightest weight, the next weight along will be heavier. This is independent of the actual weight of each weight; indeed, it is independent of the actual weights of all the weights. After all, all the weights could be randomly put in a line. Indeed, even the property of being in a line seems to organise the weights into some order, even if they were distributed randomly within the line. In fact, Russell wanted to argue that even if the weights were randomly distributed in space, that would be a relational fact about their order (or, in ordinary English, their lack of an order).

Russell wanted to go further than our spatial example suggests. Consider a more abstract description. Suppose that there are objects in the universe of different mass, and some of the same mass. Then it is a fact about these objects that some are of the same mass, and some are of different mass, and that the ones of different mass are in fact in an abstract order of greater to lesser mass. The ones with the same mass are in an equality relation with some of the others. This is independent of facts about any particular mass, or of all the masses in themselves.

CHAPTER 5

One objection to this line of argument is that there are only individual masses and space in the spatial examples and only the individual masses in the abstract examples; but this does not look a plausible response to the spatial examples, as the masses are lined up in a particular way in space or not lined up in space – they have an order in space. However, it might be argued that in the other examples, there is no further thing there, the relations between the masses. Nevertheless, Russell presents some rather elegant arguments that there is something more. He considers two views, which he calls the monadistic and the monistic view. The monadistic view is named after Leibniz's *Monadology*, which holds that the world consists of independent monads—things that change internally but do not really interact in any way (Leibniz 1998). The monistic view holds that the world is one whole and that relations are unreal because they completely separate out what is inseparable. Russell starts by quoting Leibniz on the ratios between objects with two different lengths.

To understand Leibniz's argument in the present context, we need to grasp that by subject Leibniz means substance, and by accident he means a property at a time – an attribute in my terminology. Here is the argument as it is quoted by Russell:

> *The ratio or proportion between two lines L and M may be conceived three different ways; as a ratio of the greater L to the lesser M; as a ratio of the lesser M to the greater L; and lastly, as something abstracted from both, that is as the ratio between L and M, without considering which is the antecedent, or which the consequent; which the subject, and which the object . . .In the first way of considering them, L the greater, in the second L the lesser, is the subject of that accident philosophers call relation. But which of them will be the subject in the third way of considering them? It cannot be said that both of them, L and M together, are the subject of such an accident; for if so, we should have an accident in two subjects, with one leg in*

one, and the other in the other; which is contrary to the notion of accidents. Therefore we must say that this relation, in this third way of considering it, is indeed out of the subjects; but being neither a substance nor an accident, it must be a more ideal thing, the consideration of which is nevertheless useful. (Leibniz, as quoted in Russell 1938, 222)

Leibniz means to try to stick solely to a substance/attribute Aristotelian view, which is why he calls the third way of considering the relation 'a more ideal thing'. He means it is in some sense an idealisation which does not reflect reality. It has to do with our way of considering the lines, not something in the world as it is in itself.

Russell argues that both the first and second ways of considering the relation to show that collapsing such relations into one of the relata fails. I will only quote his discussion of the first way, as the same kind of point can be made about the second way.

In the first way of considering the matter, we have 'L is (greater than M)', the words in brackets being considered as an adjective of L. But when we examine this adjective it is at once evident that it is complex: it consists, at least, of the parts greater and M, and both of these are essential. To say that L is greater does not at all convey our meaning, and it is highly probable that M is also greater [than something else]. The supposed adjective of L involves some reference to M; but what can be meant by a reference the theory leaves unintelligible. An adjective involving a reference to M is plainly an adjective which is relative to M, and this is merely a cumbrous way of describing a relation. (Russell 1938, 222)

Russell then turns to the monistic theory. The monistic theory holds that it is not L and M considered individually that contain the relation L is greater than M. Rather, it is the whole L and M which contains the relation. The relation is not a separate thing. Russell's objection to this is that L and M together do not contain L is greater than M, for a whole consisting of L and M in which M is greater than L would equally contain both items. To explain the difference between L is greater than M, and M is greater than L, we would be forced to consider L and M separately and their relation to one another. Talking of L and M as a whole does not indicate the direction of the relation between the two (Russell 1938, 224–25).

Russell was particularly interested in criticising philosophical obscurantism. A number of philosophers of his own time tried to argue that relations were unreal through some rather obscure lines of argument. He argued that implicit in their claims was an acceptance of the reality of external relations. By contrast with various obscurantist philosophers, he admired Leibniz for his clarity; but he thought that Leibniz's struggles with the reality of external relations had made it clear that it is wrong to deny the reality of external relations.

It will be worth considering whether some of the arguments that various philosophers in recent times have put against Russell's arguments for the reality of external relations are really convoluted ways of talking about external relations. Among other issues that come up is how we describe relations. If we talk about a particular builder building a house, for instance, there will be a complex series of relations between the builder and what is being built. For instance, the builder picks up a brick. The builder places the brick on another brick. Each of these events seems to involve a series of changing physical interactions (changing external relations) over time between the brick and the builder. These interactions affect both parts of what is being built and the builder. The interactions change the spatial positions of the bricks and arrange them. They affect the builder's muscles and tire her. It is not conceptual talk that makes it true that the builder is building; it is what the builder actually does.

Armstrong's Critique of Russell

Many philosophers have been inclined to agree with at least part of Russell's line of argument, but to criticise other parts of it. Let us distinguish between the description of things and things themselves. Let me also remind readers of the notion of a truth-maker. A truth-maker is the thing or things in the world that makes some statement true. The statement 'Pushkin is sitting on a chair in my room' is true if and only if the cat Pushkin is in fact sitting on a chair in my room. Russell can be understood to imply that the truth-maker for all true relational statements must include an external relation between the things related. For instance, we can see that the truth-maker of the statement above about Pushkin includes not only Pushkin and the chair, but also a relation between them.

Now consider the statement that one cat is heavier than another. Suppose it is true that Heffalump is heavier than Pushkin. If we look in the world, we will only see Heffalump and Pushkin. Suppose we also stick something on each of them indicating their weight, which is a property of each of them. There does not seem to be anything more here that is the relation between the two. While it is true that Heffalump is heavier than Pushkin, there is no truth-maker in the world apart from Heffalump and his property of weighing a certain amount, and Pushkin and her property of weighing a certain amount. David Armstrong has argued that in such cases, the relational property comes 'for free' because it follows logically from the features of the individual things that are being related. What follows logically is not an extra feature of the world. Thus, Russell is partly right and partly wrong. He is right to say that there is a relation between Heffalump and Pushkin, and that it has a direction. He is wrong to suggest that there is an extra thing in the world – the relation between Heffalump and Pushkin. For Armstrong, such relations are what he calls 'internal relations'. By this much-abused term, he does not mean anything obscure. Internal relations are merely relations that are solely a logical consequence of a true description of the individual relata and their properties.

Armstrong contrasts internal relations with external relations. External relations are not solely a logical consequence of the relata. Consider the example I mentioned earlier, of a series of weights arranged in a line in order of their weight, from lighter to heavier. As these weights are arranged in a spatial arrangement, the relations between them are not solely a logical consequence of the relata and their properties. In such a case, Russell is completely correct, as there is an additional truth-maker in the world, the arrangement in space of the relata (Armstrong 1997, 87–93). Armstrong does not mention Russell here, but it is clear that he has him in mind.

It is not clear that Armstrong is completely right. Two cats of different weight occupying the universe at a particular time will be different from just one cat occupying the universe at that time. For one thing, the two cats will have a gravitational effect on each other. This will be very slight but will still be there. Further, Heffalump will have a greater gravitational effect on Pushkin than Pushkin has on Heffalump. The cats will also be some distance apart in space – they will have a spatial relation to one another. They will have a temporal relation to one another if they are alive at distinct times, as there will be some particular temporal gap between the times in which they are alive.

Armstrong's mistake here seems to arise from just thinking of aspects of things rather than thinking of a real world in which they always have external relations to one another. However, he seems to be right that the mere fact that Heffalump's mass is greater than Pushkin's is not an additional fact to the masses of the individual cats. There is an internal relation between the masses of the two cats as well as some external relations. So, contrary to Russell, there are some internal relations.

In the case of internal relations, there is no further thing – the relation between the relata in the world, which is a part of the furniture of the world. The truth-maker is solely the individual things in the world and their properties.

Despite what I have said about Armstrong, there are two other kinds of critiques of Russell that occur in the recent literature. Following Russell's own jargon, I have called them the monadistic critique and the monistic critique. The monadistic critique is well represented by Jonathan Lowe's arguments that relational truth-makers do not exist for at least many true relational statements, and by John Heil's arguments that only internal relations are involved in causation. The monistic critique holds that some interacting things in relations constitute an ontological whole which is not reducible to the things involved and their relation to one another. After considering monadistic critiques, I will consider the case of chemical compounds to discuss whether they are ontological wholes not reducible to the relations between their parts.

Monadistic Critiques of Russell

Jonathan Lowe starts by accepting that there are relational truths, so that Russell is right about that. He accepts that that is an important insight that transformed logic. However, he argues that there are (probably) no relational truth-makers. What he means is that there is nothing in the world in addition to the two (or more) aspects of things which are related. He starts by pointing out that some truths, such as identity statements, are relational truths, but there are no relational truth-makers in the world. So, for instance, in the statement 'Bertrand the philosopher is identical with Russell the philosopher' is true, but there is no truth-maker in the world for it other than Bertrand Russell. This is correct, and makes a similar point to that made by Armstrong. A thing's identity with itself is an internal relation. Russell being named 'Bertrand', or as 'Russell', makes no addition to his being.

Lowe also turns to statements about the property of a thing at a time, such as 'Mars is red' and argues that no relational truth-maker is involved in the truth of that statement. However, we need to distinguish between properties a thing possesses per se, and properties that are a result of its interaction with light and normal human perceivers. These interaction properties seem to be clearly the result of external relations with rays of light and perceivers. To illustrate Lowe's point, 'Earth is an oblate spheroid with its own axis of rotation' is a better example. (An oblate spheroid is a sphere that is flatter at two ends and bulges at the centre.) Earth's being an oblate spheroid with a particular axis of rotation is an aspect of Earth, not a separate thing. Using Lowe's Lockean language, it is a mode of being of Earth. However, its being an oblate spheroid with its particular axis of rotation is the result of the gravitational effect of the moon and sun, Earth's inertia, its speed of rotation, and its own gravity. So, this property too is at least partly causally a result of external relations (perhaps Lowe might argue that its own gravity, and even its inertia, are modes of its being). Were these causal effects to cease, it would instantly cease to be an oblate spheroid with its particular axis of rotation.

Nevertheless, Lowe has a critique of my argument. Lowe argues by using the example of the relational statement Abelard loves Heloise. He argues that this could be true even if Heloise did not exist. Perhaps Abelard imagines Heloise to exist. A quick reply is available here. If Heloise is a figment of Abelard's imagination rather than a real person he sees and knows, there will be very different states of his brain. Further, if Heloise is not merely a figment of Abelard's imagination, Heloise's effect on Abelard will at least be part of the cause of Abelard's love. (This is not to say that Heloise is responsible for Abelard's love. Abelard may be a fantasist, and perhaps her causing an effect is only through being seen by Abelard.) So, the two situations are not causally equivalent. In any case, other examples in which imagination is not involved, like the one about Earth above, are not difficult to counter. Perhaps Earth could be an oblate spheroid with its particular axis of rotation under different gravitational conditions. But in the actual world, the influence of the moon and sun is crucial. So that is the external relation that is partly producing the shape of Earth. It is that relation that is part of the truth-maker for statements about the cause of Earth's being an oblate spheroid with its particular axis of rotation.

Lowe goes on, however, to give a powers and liabilities account of causation. I must now move on to correct some Aristotelian assumptions. It is not true, at least in many cases, that there are simply powers and liabilities. At least many cases of causation, perhaps all, are the result of interaction. When salt dissolves in water, there is a complex chemical reaction in which both the salt and the water are involved. It can be convenient to talk of powers and liabilities, but we are interested in the world, not in descriptions. Even in the case of Earth, Earth's gravitation affects the sun, and the sun in turn affects Earth. These are not separate processes. The sun's effects are intertwined with Earth's effects, including effects on itself, to produce the oblate spheroid spinning on a particular axis that is Earth. They cannot be pulled apart in time or space. Lowe seems to rely on a naïve Physics and Chemistry that dates back to Aristotle but is mistaken. It is at least not typically the case that things have powers which act on liabilities; powers interact. A simple example is walking. When we walk, our stepping on the pavement produces *at the same time* an opposite reaction as the pavement pushes back on us according to Newton's third law – every action has an equal and opposite reaction. This is what makes walking possible. Walking is interactive even though we conceive of ourselves as acting on the liability of a passive pavement. Lowe is correct to argue that powers do not require a manifestation. However, Aristotle's power/liability account needs correcting. We separate powers conceptually, but in the world, they interact to produce results.

At this point, we need to consider an argument by John Heil. Heil agrees that it is the interaction of causal powers that produces effects. Effects are the interaction of causal powers. However, he holds that the interaction of causal powers, which are essential to the things interacting, means that the things interact necessarily. Hence, an internal relation is involved between the things interacting. He argues that powers are individuated through what they manifest with a partner. However, this is misleading. Consider the power to heat. What we call 'heat' also expands things and has electrical effects, among others. We might individuate it as the power to heat, but in fact, it is something in the world that does a multiplicity of things. If we call it a power to heat, of course, conceptually that's what it does. But it is not, in fact, a power just to heat. It is a multi-faceted power, some of whose effects we have probably not yet even discovered. So, the thing itself is not individuated as the power to heat. It does a variety of things essentially in conjunction with other things. In addition, it could act with a range of reciprocal partners. Which one it acts with depends on the situation it is placed in. My walking on a specific pavement in Athens is different from my walking on a specific pavement in Adelaide, even if each pavement is made of the same materials. These relations are external. Each of them need not have happened. Of course, once I have decided to put my foot on the pavement in Athens, something necessarily happens. But it does not happen with conceptual necessity. Neither was I driven to walk in Adelaide with conceptual necessity. Heil is confusing conceptual necessity with material necessity.

It is important to note here that there are different truth-makers in different situations. The truth-maker that a pavement in Athens is producing a reaction to my putting my foot down is different from the truth-maker that a pavement in Adelaide is producing a reaction to my putting my foot down. We can point to different things in the world that are involved in the interactions. These are clearly examples of external relations, even though the power in my foot and the power of the pavements necessarily affect one another.

A Monistic Critique of Russell

Russell's criticism of monism was a criticism of the monism of the Hegelians, in which the world as a whole is one thing, and parts of it cannot be separated because what they are is dependent on the whole. It makes good sense to criticise this view. My foot and a pavement are not one thing, even though they are involved in an interaction. However, a narrower monistic critique can be used to criticise Russell. It is a consequence of Aristotle's hylomorphism as applied to Chemistry. Although water is produced by Hydrogen and Oxygen coming together in a chemical compound, the properties of the compound are different from its components. For instance, both Hydrogen and Oxygen are highly combustible, but water is not. A new thing arises in a compound. This contrasts with chemical mixtures. If I mix water and sand together, they do not form a compound. Now Russell might say that we can still distinguish the water by referring to it as a compound of Hydrogen and Oxygen. However, this seems to mean no more than that the water came from Hydrogen and Oxygen, and that we can get Hydrogen and Oxygen out of the water. No Aristotelian needs to deny this.

Russell nevertheless has a partial reply available to my Aristotelian argument in the preceding paragraph. A chemical compound is a specific kind of external (in part, spatial) relation between the atoms of the elements in the compound, some of whose properties are reducible to the atoms composing it. By contrast, the things in a chemical mixture are in an external relation, but it is like the external relation between my feet and a pavement when I am walking. We do not need to go into the scientific details here.

It is impossible to come to a definitive conclusion as to whether chemical compounds are wholes which are not reducible to the parts which underlie them in spatial relations. Some of the properties of chemical compounds are reducible to their parts in spatial relations, and others are not. That is to say, some of their properties seem to be the result of their being irreducible wholes in some respects, and some of their properties are the result of reducible relations between parts.

Conclusion

Russell is correct to say that there are true relational statements. A logic that does not deal with relational inferences between true statements is inadequate. Aristotle's logic is inadequate and needs to be supplemented by a logic that includes relational statements. However, there are some relations that are internal, so that there is no additional truth-maker in the world in such relations apart from the relata. There are also, as we have seen, external relations. In the case of external relations, there are additional truth-makers in the world. Further, some hylomorphic items are, in certain respects, wholes which are not reducible to their parts and their relations. Russell was mistaken in completely rejecting irreducible wholes.

We need to note here that naïve empiricist reluctance to admit anything we cannot see into our ontology seems to be one of the driving forces behind the attempts to deny the existence of external relations. This reluctance drives philosophers into ad hoc manoeuvres designed to get out of accepting the existence of external relations. Such manoeuvres are verbal devices which do not advance our knowledge.

An important confusion in various arguments against the existence of external relations is the confusion between two different claims: (1) an external relation might not change the internal constitution of the things being related, and (2) an external relation does not exist. It is true that it is logically possible that an external relation might not change the things being related. Nevertheless, all that shows is that an external relation can be independent of the relata. Consider a world in which a series of weights arranged in a line from heaviest to lightest does not in fact generate gravitational forces between the weights. Still, there would be a fact about the arrangement of the weights which is independent of their weight.

Russell wanted to highlight a further confusion, which is the confusion between our description of things and the actual order of things in the world. We have seen an example of such a confusion in Heil's argument above. For another example, take again the series of weights arranged from heaviest to lightest in a line in a world in which they do not generate gravitational forces on one another. I have described it that way, so you might think the relation between them is a necessary relation. But if they existed in that order, it would not be a necessary relation between them in the world or between them and space. The necessity, if it existed, would have to do with my description of them.

Further Readings

An important collection which includes key arguments I have discussed in this chapter by Jonathan Lowe, John Heil and others is in Marmodoro and Yates (2016). Anna Marmodoro has reinterpreted and defended a view Aristotle puts in Aristotle's *Physics* in Marmodoro 2014, chapter 1. She tries to save Aristotle's view that something with a power somehow points to something with a liability to that power when it affects the thing with the liability. This would leave Aristotle's rejection of external relations intact. Russell would have regarded Aristotle's argument as obscurantist rather than illuminating. Something pointing towards something else seems to be a relation between two things. If I point at my cat or if I look at my cat, I have created an external relation with my cat, which is a spatial external relation.

Chapter 6

Space

We think of things in the world as being separated by space. I am separated from my window by space. My yard is separated from the yards of my neighbours by space, and so on. You might think of the fact that science tells us that the separation between us and other things is filled with atoms and molecules of various kinds that we cannot see. Nevertheless, those atoms and molecules are separated from one another by small spaces. Some distance from the earth, the atoms and molecules in empty space become sparser and there seems to be a great deal more empty space. What is this empty space? If it is a thing, it seems to be a very strange thing indeed. Parts of it seem to have a size, but it seems that in the empty parts of this size there is nothing. Further, as things can be moved around in space to new locations, it seems that all objects are located in space – but this thing, space, seems to be only an emptiness that objects can occupy – a void. It cannot be moved around even though objects can move around in it. How could it exist? Are we making 'Much Ado About Nothing', as the title, though not the content, of an entertaining book on medieval theories of space suggests? Alternatively, is space an unusual kind of thing which will have to be added to our list of kinds of being?

CHAPTER 6

FROM MELISSUS TO ARISTOTLE

The fifth-century BCE philosopher Melissus argued explicitly for the non-existence of void space, stating that 'emptiness is nothing, and nothing cannot exist' (Waterfield 2000, 85). This must have seemed plausible to some thinkers of the time, as indeed it does today. Aristotle followed up Melissus' view by presenting a thorough account of space as something that does not really exist. Unlike relations, which he discusses to dismiss their reality as separate kinds of things, space is not a kind of being he even mentions in *Categories*, although he mentions place. His account in *Physics* holds that there is no void and that there is only the two-dimensional surface of various objects abutting one another. Place is nothing else but a two-dimensional surface abutting something else. There is really no space and no void. Aristotle introduced the influential idea of a plenum, the idea that there are no void spaces between objects. Aristotle, like many of his successors, thought that if there is a plenum, there is no space. We will see later that this is a dubious assumption.

Aristotle presented several arguments against the existence of space. I will only mention a few:

The first argument is that anything which exists is a body, and two bodies cannot interpenetrate one another. However, if space exists, there would be two bodies in the same place. As an illustration of the same point, Aristotle considers placing a wooden cube in a material medium such as air or water. It always displaces some of that medium. It cannot interpenetrate the medium. Nevertheless, if void existed, there would be nothing to displace, and it would have to interpenetrate the bodies in it. Of course, this argument merely assumes that anything which exists is a material body that we can experience, just like other material bodies. In other words, this argument presupposes a naïve empiricism about what exists.

A second argument is that space is superfluous, so that one could multiply such things without making any difference. Take the cube again. How does it add anything by saying that the cube occupies a space? If we do say that, why not multiply the number of spaces the cube occupies?

A third argument for the non-existence of space involved identifying space with a pure void. Of course, it then seems to be nothing. Aristotle argued that movement in such a void is impossible because the speed of a moving object in a void would have no mathematical ratio to the density of a medium, just as nothing does not have a ratio to a number. All motion must have such a ratio to cover a distance in a time. Aristotle then imagined that to get a ratio, we must use the ratio of a medium that is very thin. However, we would have to equate the resistance of this medium to a void which provides no resistance; but to make these equivalent is impossible because that would be to equate the resistance of a very thin medium to something that provides no resistance. So, on Aristotle's account, motion in a void is impossible. He concludes that a void cannot exist.

Aristotle's view quickly fell out of favour because of its implausibility. Various philosophers developed views which held that void space exists. In particular, the atomists thought that the best explanation for the behaviour of various things is that there are void spaces between objects – for instance, the behaviour of air is to be explained by assuming that air atoms are widely spaced and so can easily be moved apart by pushing through them.

PHILOPONUS'S CRITICISMS OF ARISTOTLE

The Byzantine philosopher John Philoponus developed some central criticisms of the Aristotelian view. To understand Philoponus's contribution, it is necessary to spell out some background. As Philoponus's milieu was heavily influenced by Aristotle and others, he accepted that there is, in fact, a plenum. Nevertheless, he argued that despite the existence of a plenum, space exists. This was a startling view, as it was assumed by both the Aristotelians and their opponents that the existence of a plenum implied that

CHAPTER 6

there is no space. Philoponus presented several arguments. I will only consider three.

First, Philoponus asks us to consider a jar which is first full of air and then filled with water. We are to assume that we are measuring the volume of the water by using the jar. On Aristotle's plenist account, the water has totally displaced the air. However, the water cannot be taking up the two-dimensional surfaces of the sides of the jar, or the surface of the water; for the water, which is a body, is taking up the space between the sides of the jar up to the surface (the water is not identical with the sides of the jar, for then it would be part of the jar). What we are trying to measure is clearly a three-dimensional volume. The space inside the jar must be this three-dimensional volume between the sides of the jar. Philoponus points out at the end of his argument that a three-dimensional volume cannot be identical with a feature of what is in it, as the contents are constantly displaced while the volume remains the same. (Philoponus 2014, 28–30).

Second, Philoponus asks us to consider a solid three-dimensional object moving through air. It displaces the air which then moves into the area vacated by the object. But if it does this, there cannot be a mere surface that the object moves into, for it is a three-dimensional object with a particular volume. So, there must be a void space vacated by air, which is a three-dimensional space with a particular volume (Philoponus 2014, 72).

Third, Philoponus pointed out that the evidence for resistance to motion by a medium only shows that it takes extra time to move through a medium than through a void. It does not show that the speed of a moving object in a void would be infinite. The speed of an object is not only dependent on the resistance of the medium, but on the impulse with which the object is travelling. So, the argument for the impossibility of a void fails. Philoponus illustrated his argument by pointing out that of two archers, one stronger than the other, it would be the stronger one who would fire an arrow further, even in a void (Philoponus 2014, 56–7).

Philoponus treated space as a thing which is a void, the immobile three-dimensional, in which all other objects were located, had a certain volume, and could be moved. For him, space is something which could exist even if there were no objects in it. A consequence of this view is that space is not a mere nothing, as it has geometrical properties. A further consequence of this view is that geometry is not a purely formal system. It is the science which studies the laws that apply to three-dimensional space. We will see later that these consequences have once again become important in recent arguments for the reality of space.

THE SEVENTEENTH-CENTURY DEBATE

Various discussions about the reality of void space occurred in the middle ages. The rediscovery of Philoponus's work in Western Europe in the sixteenth century sharpened debates and tilted opinion in favour of the existence of space. Nevertheless, in the seventeenth century, an influential debate occurred between Samuel Clarke, a follower of the great physicist Isaac Newton, and Gottfried Leibniz, the great philosopher and mathematician. It is this debate which is the origin of modern discussions of space. According to Clarke and Newton, space exists as a separate thing. It could exist even if there were no things in it. This view is often called substantivalism, for it holds that space is an unusual substance – it is a being in addition to the other beings which exist in the world. By contrast, Leibniz, who admired Aristotle and wanted to modernise his view about space, held that there were merely relations between things in the world. If there were no things, the world would have no spatial features. This view is often called relationism, for it holds that space is not an additional thing in the world; it consists of relations between things. Leibniz went on to develop his view further. It is obvious that things can be moved around in relation to each other. On his view, what we call space is not only the relations between things at a time but also all the possible relations things can have to one another.

It is important to grasp that, for those who want to deny the existence of space, Leibniz's view is a significant advance on Aristotle's. For it seems that we only rely on relations between things in measuring things or judging motion. For instance, Leibniz could criticise Philoponus's displacement argument by pointing out that all we do in judging an object (or a mass of air) to be three-dimensional is measure it in relation to other objects. The changing relations between measuring instruments and objects are all we know to be there. Thus, Leibniz could argue, we do not need to postulate a three-dimensional space independently existing when an object is being displaced. Leibniz changed the debate about space by introducing relationism to eliminate the need to postulate space as an independently existing thing.

We have seen in the previous chapter that Leibniz argued that relations do not really exist as separate beings. So, Leibniz wanted to eliminate both space and relations as separate beings from ontology. However, many modern relationists about space do not accept Leibniz's argument for the unreality of external relations while they accept some of Leibniz's arguments against substantivalism. I have criticised Leibniz's arguments against the existence of external relations in the previous chapter. Here I will only discuss his central arguments against substantivalism.

RELATIONIST ARGUMENTS AGAINST SPATIAL SUBSTANTIVALISM

Leibniz argued from two principles, the identity of indiscernibles and the principle of sufficient reason:

The first principle is the identity of indiscernibles. The principle holds that if two things are indistinguishable, they are the same thing. Leibniz applied it to space. Suppose that all the spatial relations between objects were the same, but they were moved a hundred metres away from where they are now. That situation would be no different from the situation that currently holds. Hence, following the principle, it is the same as the current situation of objects in the universe. But then there is no difference provided by the supposed absolute spatial position of objects. So, space does not exist.

The first principle may be tempting, but it is difficult to see why it must be true. That we are merely unable to tell the difference between two things does not mean that they are the same. There are many things we cannot discern. This does not mean that they do not exist. Presumably, Leibniz and his followers think the case of two identical objects is different from many other things we cannot discern. Take the question of whether there is life in the most far away galaxies. Perhaps we will never be able to tell. However, if we were there, we would be able to tell. By contrast, it seems that if two objects were indistinguishable, we would not be able to tell them apart no matter how hard we tried, and whatever scientific instruments we could use. Even God, if it existed, would have no way to tell them apart. Such objects would be truly indistinguishable – no intrinsic or relational difference would allow anyone to tell them apart.

It is hard to see why we should accept the first principle, even when it is only supposed to apply to things that are truly indistinguishable. Why should there not be things in the universe that are truly indistinguishable, like so-called identical twins but indistinguishable (so-called identical twins are distinguishable per se by tiny differences)? After all, so-called identical twins are so similar, it is very difficult to tell them apart. It only seems a short step to have genuinely indistinguishable identical objects.

The Leibnizian can, of course, reply to the argument in the last paragraph that even identical twins would have a different life-history. For instance, one is going to be born first. This would mean that their relations to other objects would be different over their life-histories. This would make them relationally distinguishable. However, a plausible reply to this argument can be produced through a thought experiment. It is logically possible, for instance, that there could be a universe in which only two intrinsically identical objects existed, such as two spheres made of exactly the same material and having exactly the same volume and shape. Suppose they are spatially distinct objects. None of their intrinsic or relational properties would distinguish them. Yet such a situation can be conceived. The fact that it can be conceived shows that the first principle is not true.

The principle of sufficient reason holds that there must be a cause why something is a particular way, for instance, there must be a cause of why the temperature today in Adelaide is over thirty degrees Celsius. Leibniz gave the principle a theological spin; he thought that as God is supremely rational, he must have a reason why the world is a particular way at a particular time. Many philosophers have not found Leibniz's theological musings convincing. However, they have thought that the principle might well be correct in a causal form. Stated in a modernised form, the principle is that there must be a cause why things are a particular way at a particular time. Now Leibniz claimed that if things had an absolute spatial location, the principle would be false. He considered examples like everything in the universe moving towards some position away from where it is now while preserving all the spatial relations between things over all of time. If this were possible, there would be no sufficient reason why everything in the universe is located where it is now located. He argued that the only way to preserve the principle of sufficient reason, which he took to be obviously true, is to assume that such a situation is impossible. Relationism implies that such a situation is impossible. So, Leibniz thought that relationism must be true.

To spell out Leibniz's view further, we must consider the whole history of the objects in the universe through time. Of course, it seems current objects are where they are because of previous causes. So, their position now is not causeless. However, if we think back to the time when they came into existence in an apparently spatially infinite universe, we can raise the question why at the early stage of the universe they were in one place rather than another. After the big bang, which started the universe and its rapid cosmic inflation, why did things end up where they are? There may well be an answer to this question provided by a future Physics, though we do not know the answer now. If there is such an answer, then we can satisfy the principle of sufficient reason without appealing to relationism. This would mean that modern Leibnizians could not appeal to the principle of sufficient reason to ground their relationism. Alternatively, there may be no sufficient cause for why things were located where they were very soon after the big bang. Perhaps the fundamental laws of nature are only probabilistic – if this were true, then the principle of sufficient reason would be false.

Let me put aside the principle of sufficient reason. Consider the following thought experiment from Henri Poincaré, who wanted to further Leibniz's case against substantivalism: What if space and everything in it were to double in size overnight? Every object doubles in size, and the spatial distance between objects doubles in size. In this scenario, apparently no measuring instrument would enable us to tell the difference, as all measuring instruments would also have doubled in size. If there would be no difference between this imaginary situation and our current situation, then there is no such thing as space. There are only the relations between objects, which, as far as we would be able to tell, would be preserved.

Before we move on, I should note something about Poincaré's argument. For it to work, we must assume that the identity of indiscernibles is true. However, as we have seen, that principle is not obviously true. Supposing we could not tell whether everything has doubled in size does not mean that there would not be a real fact of the matter in the world. Perhaps everything has doubled in size but no one will ever be able to tell. We will see that, in any case, we would be able to tell.

Chapter 6

CRITICISMS OF ARGUMENTS AGAINST SUBSTANTIVALISM
Let us start by considering Leibniz's argument that we would not be able to tell if everything in the universe were to move some distance away from where it is now while relations between things are all preserved. On behalf of Newton, Clarke pointed out that while this is true of objects moving inertially, that is, with a uniform speed in a straight line, it is not true of objects accelerating. To understand this argument, consider a bucket half-filled with water suspended on a string. Now assume the string is twisted up. When the string is released, the bucket will rotate, thereby accelerating. What will happen is that the top of the water in the bucket will form a curve. Such examples seem to show that acceleration in space is detectable even if the relations between objects remain the same. But how is it detectable if absolute motion in space does not exist, as the relationist holds?

It is possible for the Leibnizian to reply to the argument in the previous paragraph by pointing out that as the string untwists, the relations between the parts of the string are constantly changing. Hence, the relationist has a plausible reply to the argument. However, Newton presented a second argument for the same conclusion. Newton imagined two globes connected by a string between them. The globes are rotating constantly. The tension in the string, which can be measured, will show that they are rotating rather than still. Rotating globes will tend to move away from the centre of the string. By measuring the tension, we could work out that the globes are rotating, as rotation is a form of acceleration in Physics. To satisfy the relationist, we can imagine that all the other objects in the universe are moving too, so that we cannot tell by using changing relations that the globes are moving. Alternatively, we can imagine that the globes and the string are the only things in the universe.

It is difficult to see how relationists can answer the substantivalist argument in the last paragraph. Of course, it involves a thought experiment, and relationists can criticise it for using a thought experiment. However, note that relationists, starting with Leibniz, also use thought experiments. The various defences of the identity of indiscernibles involve using thought experiments. So, relationists are in no position to criticise the use of thought experiments.

Let me now turn to the everything doubling in size thought experiment. As Graham Nerlich says,

> *doubling a thing in all its lengths will quadruple its cross-sectional area and multiply its volume and thus its mass by eight. The load bearing functions of the object are essentially functions of area, but the loads they must bear for the thing to be stable are functions of its mass.* (Nerlich 1994a, 149)

What this means is that nocturnal doubling would have testable effects. Suddenly, the things in the world that were able to stand various stresses, like my desk, would be unable to support my computer as the computer would break the desk. Many such effects would be detectable. We have so far left out the fact that the size of the earth would also double. This would mean that the gravitational force exerted by the earth would be much stronger. As it follows from the relationist view that the effects of doubling would be undetectable, it seems that the relationist view must be false.

Various replies have been produced to the argument that doubling would be detectable; let me now turn to Nerlich's more powerful argument. To understand it, we need to consider the revolution in geometry that occurred in the late nineteenth and twentieth centuries. While Leibniz assumed that the only true geometry is the Euclidean geometry we learnt at school, it is now understood that other geometries of space are possible. To grasp this point in an elementary fashion, consider Playfair's axiom, which is equivalent to a crucial part of Euclidean geometry. Playfair's axiom says that if we take a line on a plane, then

CHAPTER 6

one and only one line drawn through a point elsewhere on the plane will be parallel to that line. The revolution in geometry started when geometers realised that that axiom is not obviously true and proceeded to develop geometries that deny that axiom. Some of these imaginable and coherent geometries have been used in Physics. Einstein's General Theory of Relativity, which is now well-confirmed, used a variant of one of these geometries, Riemannian geometry, to make important predictions.

In Euclidean geometry, the three angles of a triangle always add up to 180 degrees. Let us now think about Riemannian geometry. In Riemannian geometry, space, and so all lines, are positively curved. This means that the lines follow the surface of a sphere. Now suppose, as many physicists suppose, that over a certain distance, a light signal will curve in the same manner as the lines on a sphere will curve. What will happen to a triangle in such a space? It turns out that the triangle will have angles that add up to more than 180 degrees. To understand the point in a simple manner, consider the sphere of the earth. Suppose space were two dimensional and followed the surface of the sphere of the earth. Take a triangle on that surface. It will have angles that add up to more than 180 degrees. What this means is that nocturnal expansion will make a difference. The doubling of everything in the world which has Riemannian curvature will be discernibly different. Imagine an observer sending out light signals from the top of the vertices of a triangle on the surface of a sphere. One signal goes out to an observer at each end of the two vertices. Then one of the observers at one end of the vertices sends out a signal to the observer at the other end of the vertices. They use this data to measure the length of the vertices and the length of the bottom of the triangle. The measurements will be different on the surface of a sphere from those we would get on a flat surface. We would be able to tell by measuring the angles of the triangle. They would add up to more than 180 degrees. Similarly, in a three-dimensional Riemannian space, the measurements would be different from those in a three-dimensional Euclidean space. A triangle measured in that space would have angles that are more than 180 degrees.

What has gone wrong with Poincaré's doubling argument? Nerlich thinks what has gone wrong with all such arguments is that they are committed to a false thesis he calls 'the detachment thesis', which holds that 'thing-thing spatial relations are logically independent of thing-space relations' (Nerlich 1994a, 148). We can immediately see from the example of a possible Riemannian space that the thesis is false. It was not obvious to Leibniz that the thesis is false, as he simply assumed that the only geometry is Euclidean geometry. In a Euclidean space, we would indeed not be able to tell the geometrical difference between, for instance, a space that doubles in size overnight and a space that does not. An advantage of spatial substantivalism is that it can explain simply the varied and testable features of various spatial geometries.

Physicists have found good evidence that the geometry of space varies depending on whether various very massive objects are present. Around a very massive object, space will apparently curve. Very precise tests have confirmed the prediction, which is a consequence of the curvature of space. Where there is no very massive object nearby, space will be Euclidean or near Euclidean. This is a consequence of the General Theory of Relativity, which I have mentioned above.

I have dealt with some arguments for relationism as well as presented some arguments against relationism through examining relationist arguments carefully. I will next turn to some further arguments against relationism.

Further Arguments Against Relationism

The first argument against relationism is that relationists need to explain not only actual, but also possible relations. What makes certain relations possible? An obvious answer is the nature of space. The structure of space makes some relations possible and others not possible. For instance, if space is positively curved, there cannot be a Euclidean straight line between two objects. But this answer is not available to relationists as they deny the existence of space. Relationists owe us an account of what grounds the possibility of certain relations but not others.

In the eighteenth century, Kant put an important second argument against relationism. To understand that argument, it is necessary to start with some examples. Certain things have a spatial orientation in space such that they cannot be rotated into the opposite orientation. Take a right-hand glove. No matter how you try, you cannot rotate it so that it becomes a left-hand glove. The handedness of the glove seems to be a feature of its orientation in space. To understand this point, it is useful to consider a mirror image of yourself wearing a right-hand glove. The mirror image shows you wearing a left-hand glove. Yet no matter what you do in the real world, you cannot make a right-hand glove a left-hand glove. Kant identified many other examples of this phenomenon. Screws screw into nuts with a particular orientation. A screw will not fit into a nut with the opposite orientation, and so on.

Kant noted that if we take the objects by themselves, the relations of the parts of the objects to one another seems to be the same as for objects oriented the other way. For instance, the relations between the fingers and thumb of a right-hand glove are the same as the relation of the fingers and thumb of a left-hand glove to one another. Yet the two gloves are importantly different (Kant 1968).

Objects, such as some drawings, which can be rotated into the opposite orientation are called congruent counterparts of one another. Objects which cannot be rotated into the opposite orientation are called incongruent counterparts. A right-hand glove of the same size and the same internal angles as a left-hand glove is an incongruent counterpart of the left-hand glove.

It should be noted that there would also be incongruent counterparts in two-dimensional space. To see this, take the letters b and d (in lower case in this font). Cut out a piece of paper with each letter and place it on a flat table. You cannot turn each letter into its incongruent counterpart letter by just moving them around flat on the table. You would have to rotate one of the letters in three-dimensional space to make them congruent. Then a b could become a d and vice versa. Try it and you will see that I am right. This is an extraordinary fact which is not easy to explain on a relationist view. Based on this fact, Ludwig Wittgenstein argued that in a four-dimensional space, a right-hand glove could be turned into a left-hand glove just by rotating it in a four-dimensional space. We can apparently conclude from this that the dimensionality of space makes some things into incongruent counterparts.

It is now easy to see where Kant's line of argument is going. Take a right-hand glove. It will only fit into a right-hand space in a three-dimensional space. Similarly, a b would only fit into a b-shaped space in a two-dimensional space. We apparently have an argument that space itself has orientation properties that depend on its dimensionality.

In response, relationists might say that the orientation of a right-hand glove is only there in relation to a left-hand glove. But it seems logically possible that a universe should exist that only contains a right-hand glove. If this is logically possible, the glove's handedness seems to have to do with the nature of space. Again, this is a thought experiment, but relationists are not able to object to thought experiments as they use them themselves.

Relationists can, of course, produce another reply to the substantivalist. It is that the orientation is built into the gloves themselves. However, this reply is very implausible in the light of the fact that there is a good argument that handedness depends on the dimensionality of the space in which it is embedded. We have seen that a b can be turned into a d, and vice versa, in a three-dimensional space, whereas such a rotation apparently cannot be accomplished in a two-dimensional (flat) space. This gave us a good reason to follow Wittgenstein in thinking that a right-hand glove could be rotated into a left-hand glove in four-dimensional space. Taking space to be a real thing that is part of the cause of the orientation of objects gives a simple explanation of handedness, while relationism must provide contrived explanations of the phenomenon.

Conclusion

The intuition that space is a mere void and that such a void cannot exist is one driving force behind various forms of relationism. Yet we have known since the time of Philoponus that substantivalists do not claim that space is a mere nothing. It is something that is structured. It is, at least at the everyday level, something which is like a three-dimensional Euclidean structure in which other things are located, take up three-dimensional spatial properties, and can be moved around.

Another driving force behind various varieties of relationism is the view that space itself is unobservable. However, in this respect, it is no different from many entities described by science whose existence and properties are not observable but have to be inferred from other observables. These include gravity, plausibly explained in Modern Physics through the curvature of space. Would anyone deny the existence of gravity? Nevertheless, various attempts have occurred in the history of science to deny that gravity is a genuine thing that affects things at a distance. For instance, Descartes, who denied the existence of space, postulated that gravity was caused by tiny particles in a vortex that swept the planets in orbits around the sun. He postulated the vortex to eliminate an entity he thought to be so strange that it could not exist. While early relationists denied the existence of gravity as some kind of force and postulated vortices and the like, modern relationists do not postulate any such thing – yet when they eliminate space, they have no plausible explanation for the measurable force that can be detected. By contrast, the substantivalist has a plausible explanation for the origin of that force. It is to be explained because it is a feature of the curvature of space, as I noted above in discussing the General Theory of Relativity.

A central point in favour of substantivalism is that it can explain a range of phenomena, such as the ones I have discussed above, without ad hoc manoeuvres. By contrast, the relationist must postulate different and rather contrived explanations for different cases. The relationist must also rely on principles that seem to have no basis, like the identity of indiscernibles.

Further Readings

The central text which summarises the key arguments from various points of view, and adds valuable explanations, is Dainton (2010). Dainton also goes well beyond what I cover by introducing the notion of space-time. He explains the Theory of Relativity very clearly and discusses its implications thoroughly. He provides a clear explanation of how gravity is explained through the cuvature of space-time. Dainton's book is already a classic accessible treatment of philosophical issues concerning space and time.

Sklar (1982) is a very clear summary of various arguments and puts a case for relationism. Nerlich (1994b) is the central substantivalist treatment of the issues I have discussed. However, it is a difficult work.

Philoponus's contribution is discussed by Sedley and others in Sorabji (1987). Grant (1981) is an amusing discussion of medieval theories of space and the vacuum, which were influenced by Aristotle. He also traces the importance of the arguments of Philoponus in the early modern period. Many of the medieval debates prefigure modern debates.

CHAPTER 7

Distance, Motion and Change of Place

Zeno of Elea is a fifth-century BCE Greek philosopher who propounded several paradoxical arguments against the existence of motion and plurality. Zeno seems to have been defending a view of the Greek philosopher Parmenides that there is really no change. There is neither alteration nor change of place. There is also no distance between anything because there is only one thing. Aristotle confronted these arguments, arguing that they are all fallacious, but that we learn lessons about size, distance and change from solving them. On Aristotle's account, change and alteration are real. There is also a real distance between objects, and objects have a real size.

Aristotle also treated Zeno's arguments as if they were arguments for a kind of atomism, an atomism that claimed that distances, objects and changes came in an infinite number of parts.

A crucial part of Aristotle's solutions to Zeno's paradoxes is the claim that motion, distance, objects and time do not come in minimal parts. They can be subdivided into smaller and smaller intervals, but they do not consist of minimal atomic parts. Further, although they can, in a sense, be divided anywhere, they cannot be divided everywhere at the same time.

Variants of Aristotle's solutions to Zeno's paradoxes were widely accepted until the nineteenth century. Developments in mathematics then allowed solutions to the problems which did assume that distances and things consisted of atomic parts, zero-sized points. Motions could also be taken to consist of static components. Bertrand Russell, who rejected Aristotle's solutions, praised Zeno for his insight and argued that the paradoxes 'are not . . . foolish quibbles: they are serious arguments raising difficulties which it has taken two thousand years to answer' (Russell 1926, 175). However, Russell thought that the problems had been decisively solved in the late nineteenth century by producing a consistent and coherent account of how distances could consist of zero-sized points and motion could consist of a series of static events.

An important problem in Metaphysics is whether Aristotle or Russell is right. Can distances consist of atomic parts, or do they consist of intervals? Indeed, as I have argued that space is real, does space consist of zero-sized points, or is it one thing that can be thought of for convenience as broken up into intervals? Are material objects really constituted out of zero-sized points? Are objects in motion really a series of static events bound together, or should motion be understood in a different manner? To tackle these questions, I will only discuss three of Zeno's paradoxes: the dichotomy, the paradox of plurality, and the paradox of the arrow.

THE THREE PARADOXES

The dichotomy is easy to explain. Zeno argued that to move over a distance, even the smallest one, we must first cover half the distance, then a quarter of the distance, then an eighth of the distance, then a sixteenth of the distance, and so on to the end of the distance. This means we must complete an infinite number of tasks, which is impossible. So, motion is impossible. As Russell understood this paradox, it also involves crossing an infinite number of points. We can see this if we think completing each component of the distance involves walking or running over points. As there are an infinite number of components of the distance, we must be crossing an infinite number of points. (Russell would have added that each component of the run is composed of an infinite number of points.)

The explanation of the paradox of plurality in Aristotle is vague. I will instead use the account of the sixth-century philosopher, Simplicius. Take a material object, such as my desk. It can be divided and divided again to infinity. At its smallest, the desk must either consist of parts of no size (mathematical points) or it must consist of parts of some non-zero size. If it consists of parts of no size, it cannot have any size, for 0+0+0 . . . = 0. If it consists of parts of some size, then, however small they are, they will add up to something infinitely large, which is impossible – no ordinary thing is infinitely large.

The paradox of the arrow is a little harder to understand. Take an arrow in flight. At any instant, it must occupy an area equal to itself. Everything which occupies an area equal to itself is at rest. Hence, motion consists of instants of rest. However, this is impossible. So, motion is impossible.

Aristotle's Solutions to the Paradoxes

To deal with the dichotomy paradox, Aristotle points out that the times something takes to travel a distance can also be divided in the same way as the distance. So, to travel half the distance will take half the time, and so on. So, suppose that it takes a minute to walk across a room; it will take half a minute to walk half the distance, a quarter of a minute to walk a quarter of the distance, and so on. Part of what is behind this point is that 1/2 + 1/4 + 1/8 . . . add up to 1, a finite number. So, even though there is an infinite number of parts in the addition, a finite time will allow us to cover the distance. Aristotle comments that things are called infinite in two ways. Something can be infinite in divisibility or can be infinite in extension. They are not the same. Distances and times are infinite in divisibility. But this does not mean that they are infinite in extension.

Chapter 7

Modern commentators would point out that the series in the last paragraph is a series that diminishes in size as the walker proceeds. A series of tasks that diminishes in this way can be completed in a finite time, even if the number of tasks is infinite. However, a series of tasks that is not diminishing in this way cannot be completed. For instance, suppose some running track is 100 meters long; a run on it could be completed in a finite time, even if someone is very slow. However, an imaginary track that is 100+100+100+100 . . . to infinity could not be started and completed in a finite time.

Nevertheless, Aristotle wants to add a crucial point to his solution to the dichotomy and similar paradoxes. He wants to distinguish between something being divisible in any number of places and something being divided in all those places. A walk, or a run, is divisible anywhere. We could, for instance, stop halfway across a room. This doesn't mean that a walk or a run is divisible everywhere or divisible into an infinite number of parts. Aristotle thinks that is impossible. This claim seems to contradict Aristotle's initial claim about the dichotomy, but it is consistent with it if we focus on the fact that walk or run is continuous in the ordinary sense of 'continuous'. We only divide it in the imagination. Even if we stop in a number of places, we do not stop in an infinite number of places.

Aristotle's solution to the paradox of plurality is ingenious. It relies on the distinction between being divisible anywhere and being divisible everywhere. It also relies on a feature of geometry. Geometrical points are of zero size and cannot be contiguous to one another as they have no sides. Aristotle says of Zeno's argument

> let us now show that it conceals a false inference, and where this false inference lies. Since no point is contiguous to another point, the divisibility throughout of a body is possible in one sense, but not in another sense. When such divisibility is

> *postulated, it is generally held that there is a point both anywhere and everywhere in it, so that it follows that magnitudes must be divided until nothing is left. For, it is urged, there is a point everywhere in it, so that it consists either of contacts or of points. But divisibility-throughout is possible only in the sense that there is one point anywhere within it and that all its points taken separately are within it; but there are not more points than one anywhere in it (for the points are not 'consecutive'), so that it is not divisible throughout; for then if it was divisible at its centre, it will be also be divisible at a contiguous point. But it is not; for one moment in time is not contiguous to another, nor is one point to another. So much for division and composition. Hence . . . dissociation occurs into small, or relatively small, parts, while association occurs out of relatively small parts. (Aristotle 1955, 183; 317a 3–18)*

What is behind these remarks is that Aristotle thinks that material objects are not composed of points, even if we can create points on them by dividing things up. Even a line on a surface cannot be composed of points, though we can designate points on it. For a line or surface to be composed of points, he thinks that the points would have to be next to one another, but that is impossible.

Aristotle means to complete the resolution of the other part of the paradox of plurality by arguing that although we can proceed indefinitely cutting up an object into parts, we never reach point-like parts. We only reach smaller and smaller intervals. Proceeding indefinitely is not proceeding to infinity.

Aristotle's solution to the arrow paradox is stated very briefly. It is simply that time and movement do not consist of instants, so that the problem does not arise. What he means is that time and movement consist of intervals. No matter how short a time we can pick out, it will still be a time in which the arrow is like a blurry image rather than an instantaneous snapshot. The arrow never is in a precisely bounded place.

Chapter 7

Modern Developments

In the nineteenth century, developments in mathematics made it possible to talk of a line and spaces of various kinds being composed of points. Talk about infinity was also made more precise, and different infinities were described.

Let us return to Aristotle. On the modern account, Aristotle was right to emphasise that between any two points on a line or in space, no matter how close together, there are always more points – there is, indeed, an infinite number of points, something Aristotle would not have accepted because he did not believe there are any infinities. This is the property called 'denseness' in modern mathematics.

Modern geometry uses representations of real-numbered points to describe spaces, such as lines. The lines in question are real number lines. The real numbers are the rationals plus the irrational numbers. The irrational numbers are not expressible as the ratio of two natural numbers (1, 2, 3 …); they cannot be expressed as fractions. Look at the following line and the numbers above it (figure 7.1):

Suppose the line represents points out of which it is composed. The $\sqrt{2}$ and π are points designated by irrational numbers, and the others are points designated by rational numbers. Suppose this line represents points in space. Suppose that all rational and irrational numbers (even though you cannot see them on the line I have drawn) designate points. Now it would seem that all the points making up a line are represented, contrary to Aristotle. The reason is that in Physics, we use both rational and irrational numbers to describe the path of something in motion, but we apparently do not need to use any other numbers.

Arguably, then, we do not need other points to represent a line. Similarly, we can apparently describe a whole space by

$$\underline{0 \quad 1 \quad \sqrt{2} \quad 2 \quad 3 \quad \pi \ldots}$$

Figure 7.1 The Real Number Line. Source: Created by the author

Distance, Motion and Change of Place

including all the real-numbered points composing the space. By adding the irrationals to compose the line or space, we have added what modern mathematicians call 'continuity' to denseness. Continuity in this sense does not mean 'continuity' as it is normally used, for 'continuity' in the mathematicians' sense consists of something discrete.

Now you might think that perhaps this is right, but it is still the case that adding zero-sized things together adds up to zero, no matter how many zeros in an order there are to represent space. Surely, you might think, Aristotle is right to think that while we can number a point in space, space cannot be composed of points? To see that this is problematic, let us consider developments pioneered by the mathematician George Cantor. Consider two series of numbers. Take the series of numbers increasing by a quarter each time ¼, ½, ¾, 1/1, and so on. It turns out that Cantor was able to show that this series is of the same size as the natural numbers, 1, 2, 3, 4, and so on. To see this in a simple manner, put the each of the natural numbers above each of the numbers increasing by a quarter (figure 1.2):

You can see that the two series must have the same number of members, even though there are other numbers besides in the series increasing by a quarter. This is a startling result. It turns out it applies to all the rational numbers. They can all be put into one-to-one correspondence with the natural numbers. I will not explain the details here as it takes us away from the key points in this chapter. Cantor described numbers of numbers in a series as sets of numbers, collections of numbers. Any set of numbers which can be put into one-to-one correspondence with the natural numbers has the size he called aleph zero. It is denumerable,

$$1 \quad 2 \quad 3 \quad 4...$$

$$¼ \quad ½ \quad ¾ \quad 1...$$

Figure 1.2 One to One Correspondence. Source: Created by the author

which means that you could count off the numbers on a line or in a space that consists solely of rationally numbered points. Even though the number of rationals between, say, 0 and 1 is infinite, it is a denumerable infinity. In principle, the points designated by the numbers can all be counted and added up. So, denumerable infinities of points have just the property Zeno and Aristotle ascribed to them, namely that any number of them in an order add up to something of zero size. However, we have seen that to represent a space by numbering points, we would need the real numbers, which include the irrationals.

Cantor was able to show that the real numbers are not denumerable. They cannot be counted by using the natural numbers; for there are always missing numbers whenever we try to put them in one-to-one correspondence with the natural numbers. He was able to show that an infinity of real numbers is a larger, uncountable infinity than the infinity of rational numbers. As this infinity is uncountable, there is no answer that can be given about the size of an interval consisting of real-numbered points by arithmetical addition. We will need to use another method. I cannot go into the details here. Nevertheless, what this means is that a space, line or an object, consisting of an infinity of zero-sized points can have a positive size. So, although Aristotle was insightful, he was wrong in thinking that some object cannot be geometrically composed of zero-sized points. It is geometrically possible for an object or a line, or indeed, space, to be composed of zero-sized points. Whether it is physically possible remains to be discussed; for, after all, to show that something is logically possible does not show that it is physically possible.

Modern Solutions to Zeno's Paradoxes
Bertrand Russell, and later Adolf Grünbaum, presented some arguments that Zeno's paradoxes can be solved by assuming that spaces and lines are composed of zero-sized points. Russell did not apply his analysis to material objects. In the case of time, they

argued that the paradox of the arrow can be solved by assuming that time is composed of zero-sized instants. Russell made a mistake by arguing that assuming space and time consist of denumerable points would allow him to solve the paradoxes. However, Grünbaum corrected him on this claim, and on the claim about material objects. He also applied the account more widely, as we will see.

Let us discuss the paradoxes. I will start in reverse order with the paradox of the arrow. Russell said that in

> *a continuous motion . . . at any given instant the moving body occupies a certain position, and other instants it occupies other positions; the interval between any two instants and between any two positions is always finite, but the continuity of the motion is shown by the fact that, however near together we take the two positions and the two instants, there are an infinite number of positions still nearer together, which are occupied by instants which are still nearer together. The moving body never jumps from one position to another, but always passes by a gradual transition through an infinite number of intermediaries. At a given instant it is where it is, like Zeno's arrow; but we cannot say it is at rest at the instant, since the instant does not last for a finite time, and there is not a beginning or end of the instant with an interval between them. Rest consists in being in the same position at all the instants throughout a certain finite period, however short. (Russell 1926, 142)*

So, in this passage, Russell accepted Zeno's argument that at any instant the arrow occupies a precise interval, but rejected Zeno's conclusion that this shows that motion is impossible. He relied in this passage on the fact that instants are of zero size to deny that the arrow is at rest in the instant. Note that he gives an account of both motion and rest which relies on what is the case at nearby points and instants. Without the nearby points and nearby instants, it would make no sense to say that the arrow is in motion or at rest. As we will see later, however, Russell refused to commit himself as to whether treating time as consisting of instants and space as consisting of points is a true account of the world or merely a useful one. He also did not claim that material objects consist of points.

Let us turn to the paradox of plurality. We need nearby points in an order to give the standard modern account of a line or a space. A single point cannot compose anything. Nevertheless, the solution to the paradox in the modern account is now obvious. A line or a space can be composed of denumerable and non-denumerable zero-sized points in an order, none of which is right next to one another – they cannot be right next to one another as there is always an infinity of points between two points, no matter how close together they are.

Let us turn to the dichotomy. I noted that there were really two problems involved in the dichotomy:

The first one is about adding together an infinite number of intervals. Aristotle solves this by arguing that we can divide the time in the same way as we can divide the intervals. However, Aristotle doesn't think that there can be an actual infinite number of intervals, as this would mean that the walk or run has been divided into an infinite number of parts. To see why Aristotle's solution might be thought to be inadequate, let's adapt an example from David Bostock (Aristotle 1996, lxi). Suppose it takes a minute to complete a walk across a room. Now suppose we stop for half a minute at the halfway mark, a quarter of a minute after completing a further quarter of the distance, and so on. Bostock calls this 'the staccato run'. Aristotle wants to deny that the staccato run is possible as we would be completing an infinite number of actual tasks. Yet, if our original task took one minute, it seems that this task should just take two minutes, given his solution to the dichotomy (we leave aside here whether in fact we would be

Distance, Motion and Change of Place

able to time smaller and smaller intervals of time and measure smaller and smaller intervals of space. The argument is about logical possibility, not empirical possibility). Modern solutions to the dichotomy paradox do not suffer from the same problem as Aristotle's solution. They allow the addition of an infinite number of parts.

Let us turn to the second problem. Could a walker or runner cover an infinite number of points in covering the distance? According to modern solutions to this problem, she could. After all, we have seen that we can add an infinite number of zero-sized points designated by real numbers to make up something which is not of zero size.

Comparing Solutions

Several eminent modern mathematicians and philosophers, such as Gödel, Weyl, Pierce and Whitehead, have found the modern solution unproblematic as a calculating device for Physics but inadequate as an account of space, bodies, movement and time. Recently, a number of philosophers, following the lead of Whitehead, have produced accounts of these items that use intervals rather than sets of points (Arntzenhuis 2008). In the 1960s, a consistent mathematical account was produced that allows space, time and motion to consist of infinitesimals. In the current context, an infinitesimal is a thing of a size smaller than the smallest real number but is not of zero size. Leibniz's calculus, which was used in Physics until late in the nineteenth century, used infinitesimals, but it was logically inconsistent. Physicists worked out ad hoc methods for dealing with the problem, but the issue was not resolved until a consistent theory of infinitesimals was produced. I cannot spell out the details of these accounts here. It is sufficient for our purposes that they exist. We have three ways of dealing with Zeno's paradoxes consistently. First, to use intervals that can be divided, but not to infinity, which is an adaptation of Aristotle's solution. Second, to assume things consist of zero-sized points. Third, to assume they consist of infinitesimals. Let me now turn to the metaphysical issues. There are several objections that have been put to the standard modern account.

First, it has been argued that points, no matter how many there are, cannot do the same work as intervals. Points are a kind of scaffolding on intervals. The standard reply to this is that there are an infinite number of points between any two points, no matter how close together. However, since no two points that succeed each other can be next to each other, it is hard to see how this can make any difference. Points in succession would still apparently have gaps, even if they were points designated by real numbers. How strong is this objection? After all, the real numbers are sufficient for Physics. It might be the case that things in the world, including movements, might have gaps in their various stages, or parts, like a series of cinema images, only flashing on for zero time in the case of parts of movement which are at an instant. This, of course, does violence to our strong intuition that nothing can happen in no time. Unless there is some good reason to accept it, we should not accept it.

A second problem related to the first problem is that if time consists of instants and the arrow is at different instants at different times, this seems to be an unnecessary multiplication of entities. Postulating an infinite number of instants seems unnecessary by comparison to a view in which a single continuous (in the ordinary sense) time exists. Further, if the arrow is at different places at different instants, and these instantaneous arrows exist, it seems that we are now multiplying arrows to infinity. A similar issue occurs with the modern solution to the paradox of plurality. We seem to be postulating an infinity of things to solve a problem when we might just as well postulate one thing to solve the problem. It is perhaps conceivable that time and space might consist of such things, but there seems to be no reason to believe it.

A third problem is that what is postulated by some modern solutions to the paradoxes is not testable. We cannot perceive zero-sized instants because they are of zero size. We cannot perceive the points that make up space because they are of zero size, no matter how far we drill down. We have no scientific instruments that will allow us to perceive the world at this level. We also cannot perceive any effects points and instants have, as any effects they have are indistinguishable from a modernised Aristotelianism about intervals, or, indeed, from treating objects as made up of infinitesimals.

A fourth problem is that it is hard to see how points can actually be the components of material objects, even if there are an infinite number of them. Material objects come in different kinds, but points are undifferentiated by their nature. There are no iron points or silver points. Points seem to be geometrical objects that we arrive at by abstraction and idealisation. Aristotle's view about lines, spheres and other geometrical objects, which has been mentioned in chapter 4, seems correct. We have seen that there may be no spheres, yet we can do calculations with geometrical spheres that will allow us to predict the behaviour of near-spherical objects to a high degree. Of course, we also need to take account of what the objects are made of. A cricket ball is importantly different from a ball bearing made of steel. Geometry will only tell us about its approximate shape, but other features of it are also crucial in predicting its behaviour. Geometry is indifferent to constituent materials. Treating a material object as consisting of points is a geometrical treatment of a material object. As Galen Strawson says, 'If one is being metaphysically straight, the intuition that nothing (concrete, spatio-temporal) can exist at a mathematical point because there just isn't any room, is rock solid' (Strawson 2006, 16).

It is possible to respond to this fourth problem by arguing that perhaps space is constituted by points, and time by instants, even if material objects are not constituted of these things. However, we have seen that this is a profligate view which should not be accepted unless there is a good reason to accept it. Otherwise, it is just a useful calculating device. In any case, my chapter on space has argued that space is a material thing, even if it is a material thing of a rather strange kind. Russell admitted that there was no way of telling whether space is composed of points or time is composed of instants, saying

> [F]ormally, mathematics adopts an absolute theory of space and time, i.e. it assumes that besides the things which are in space and time, there are also entities called 'points' and 'instants', which are occupied by things. This view, however, although advocated by Newton, has long been regarded by mathematicians as merely a convenient fiction. There is, so far as I can see, no conceivable evidence either for or against it. It is logically possible, and it is consistent with the facts. . . . Hence, in accordance with Occam's razor, we shall do well to abstain from either assuming or denying points and instants. (Russell 1926, 153)

Conclusion

We saw in chapter 4 that calculating devices can be useful even if they do not accurately represent what is real. Idealising balls as spheres, ignoring friction, treating things as points, even when you know they cannot be points, are all useful devices for calculation; but we do not believe that they represent the world as it is. We have been given no good reason to think that representing spaces and objects through points, and times through instants is a correct representation of reality. Aristotle's view that everything that exists can be broken up into intervals, but not into points or instants, continues to be plausible, despite some problems.

Further Readings

Aristotle's principal treatment of Zeno's paradoxes is in Book 6 of his *Physics* (Aristotle 1996, 161–62; 239b 5 – 240a 18). Simplicius's important account of the paradoxes is in

Waterfield 2000, 69–81. Dainton (2010) has a very thorough discussion of the metaphysical issues raised by Zeno's paradoxes and various solutions to those paradoxes. Dainton's chapters contain an accessible and detailed account of Cantor's innovations and of relevant geometrical theories. Russell (1926) is a very interesting and accessible account of the modern solutions. Grünbaum (1967) is a thorough defence of the modern solutions. He corrects Russell on an important point. Unlike Russell, Grünbaum commits himself to the view that the standard modern mathematical view is a true account of the world.

CHAPTER 8

God

An ancient and recurring topic in Metaphysics is whether there is any evidence for the existence of a god. I will not focus on the peculiarities of the Judaeo-Christian god here. Instead, I will focus on the issue of whether there is any need to postulate an extremely intelligent and very powerful supernatural divine being to explain something about the world. By 'supernatural' I mean beings that are other than the beings which explain ordinary processes of nature in natural science, such as the behaviour of black holes, suns, electrons, and so on. I will start by turning to the ancient Greek world to see why it was thought that there was a need to postulate a god or gods. This is important as we will see that there was some reason at the time to believe in such entities. After this, I will turn to more modern times to see whether there continue to be good reasons to believe that there is a god. I will argue that the reasons the ancients had for believing in such beings vanished with the progress in modern science. I will then turn to considering some recent arguments for the existence of a god. I will only be considering arguments for the existence of a god that arise from scientific work or through metaphysical work strongly connected to natural science.

Chapter 8

The Ancient Greek World

Aristotle, perhaps the greatest and certainly the most scientifically informed philosopher of antiquity, thought that there were gods. It is worth sketching why he and others thought this by putting his view in an ancient context in order to see why there is now apparently no good reason to believe in such entities.

For the ancient Greeks, it was puzzling that the things in the heavens seemed to have such regular and mathematically predictable movements and did not seem to decay and change over centuries. (Celestial phenomena that seemed to indicate change were wrongly thought to be meteorological. The careful calculations that showed they were not meteorological were devised much later in the history of western science.) Things down in the terrestrial world clearly are subject to decay and change – their changes also seemed to be less predictable and less mathematically tractable. The mechanics of change in the world below the moon only began to be understood much later.

Aristotle thought that it was reasonable to take the way in which things appeared to the great mass of the population seriously, as well as the views of the wise. A common view held by the wise and the wider population was that the heavens were the realm of gods. This would explain the peculiarities of the heavens. Aristotle postulated that the heavens consisted of a substance not found on earth, aether. There were also gods propelling heavenly spheres, which explained the movement of the stars and planets.

Aristotle also faced another problem which came from his ancient Physics. This is that he thought, on the basis of everyday observation, that movement and change would come to an end, unless something was giving them the power to continue. For instance, cats give rise to cats which give rise to cats, and so on. The individual cats die but continually reproduce themselves. Moving objects tend to come to a stop, seemingly because they exhaust the power to move within them. But then other objects can always be made to move. How is all this possible? Aristotle postulated that there was an immaterial being, the prime mover, that the gods were trying to imitate. In turn, things on earth were trying to imitate these gods as much as possible. This was what generated a continuation of movement and patterned change in the biological world.

Aristotle did not think that his prime mover god was interested in our world. Quite reasonably, he thought that his prime mover contemplated itself and the order in the universe. This makes good sense. It is hard to see why, if there were such an entity which is so vastly superior to us, it would bother to take an interest in the welfare of vastly inferior creatures like human beings – they would differ from it in a greater way than we do from single-celled bacteria. We can see from understanding Aristotle that a Judaeo-Christian god who is deeply interested in the welfare of human beings is very unlikely, even if we think that a supernatural being plays a crucial role in the world.

In the fourth century BCE, a short time before Aristotle, Xenophon gave a reason for believing in a divine being that he claimed he heard from Socrates (Xenophon 1923, 55–65). Unlike Aristotle's divine being, this being would have to be an intelligent designer of things in the world. Xenophon noted that human and animal bodies were superbly crafted for survival and reproduction. Every major part of them seemed to have a function. He thought this implied that there had to be a god who designed them and put them into motion.

At about the same time as Xenophon, Plato, Aristotle's teacher, had proposed a divine craftsman to explain both the order in the heavens and the apparent structuring for an end of biological organisms (Plato 2000). In the second century CE, the doctor Galen added a great deal of detail to such arguments (Schiefsky 2007). These observations added some reason for believing that a divine being, if there is one, is interested in the welfare of living things in the world – though it did not make human beings special, as the Judaeo-Christian view does.

Chapter 8

By contrast to Xenophon, Plato and Galen, Aristotle thought there was no need for a designer god. In his picture of the world, living beings had always reproduced their kind going back infinitely in time. There was no time when our world with its living organisms came into being. The regularity and stability in the world had always been there. This raises two important questions we will return to later when they appear in a newer form – is there any need to postulate an originating principle of order in the universe at all? and, is a common tendency to postulate such a principle in the form of a divine designer merely the result of an unreasonable extrapolation from the order humans bring to the world?

Aristotle rejected a theory proposed by the early philosopher Empedocles, according to which the earth gave rise to random body parts. Those body parts occasionally had been put together in a way that aided the survival of creatures. Everything else died. Empedocles may have been trying to explain the origin of myths, such as the myth of the minotaur, which supposedly combined the head of a bull with the body of a man. Apart from the fact that no one had seen the earth produce any such things, Aristotle pointed out that existing species would have to have in them an ability to produce a reproductive seed to explain the continuity of species. He thought that Empedocles' story was absurd.

A version of Empedocles' story was put forward by Epicurus in the third century BCE. It involved the use of an ad hoc hypothesis. According to that hypothesis, the reason why the earth no longer produces such things is because the earth has become too old to bear these randomly produced body parts. Pretty obviously, this hypothesis looked too absurd to be taken seriously.

In the sixth century CE, John Philoponus removed the divinity of the visible heavens. He postulated that things in the heavens and on earth had regular patterns of movement, stability, and change. After all, Aristotle's story would put a kind of desire to imitate in all things apart from the prime mover; and there was no evidence of the existence of such desires. However, Philoponus could not conceive of a source of regular movement, stability and change. So, he argued that the Christian god was keeping everything going – he provided an unending power that he was putting into the world. Of course, the idea that the Christian god was doing all of this went way beyond the physical evidence. A source of power and stability might not be an intelligent being at all. But, it was reasonable given what was known, to think that there had to be some source of continuing immense power which was very different from the things we know through experience (Sorabji 1990).

In addition to the Christian god providing the power, Philoponus argued that the world had come into being at a particular time and that the Christian god had designed the features of the world, including the well-functioning structure of biological organisms. We have seen that these features of biological organisms suggested an intelligent designer being or beings. Of course, Philoponus was going well beyond the evidence to say that the designer and powering being is the Christian god.

The World of Modern Science

Let us skip to modern times. It is now understood that the same laws operate on earth and in the heavens. The heavens and the earth are also made out of the same kinds of materials and are subject to the same kind of decay. It is also now understood that energy is merely transferred from one place to another. It does not exhaust itself in motion or change. There is no need for an outside power to keep things going or to be a source of change or stability.

It has become clear through research in paleontology that well-adapted biological organisms have not existed forever. This has undermined Aristotle's view that the kinds of organisms in the world go back indefinitely in time, reproducing of their kind. However, this has not provided a boon for arguments to a designer. Darwin and Wallace have provided an account of how biological organisms come to be adapted that does not rely on a divine designer. In its modern form, it holds that there are mutations and a process of natural selection of mutations which weeds out non-beneficial mutations and promotes beneficial mutations. Over the very long run, we end up with organisms that are highly adapted to survive and reproduce. This is a considerable improvement on the crude theories of Empedocles and Epicurus. The production of mutations and their effects has been very carefully studied, as have the effects of natural selection. I will take the Darwinian account for granted in the rest of this chapter, as it is now a well-established scientific account.

David Hume's Arguments

While in the medieval period and the post-medieval period, a belief in the Judaeo-Christian god was widely accepted, this belief was increasingly brought into question in the early modern period. In his influential *Dialogues Concerning Natural Religion*, Hume put into the mouth of the sceptical Philo a whole range of arguments to undermine purported evidence for the existence of a god. A number of the arguments are directed against claims for the Judaeo-Christian god – the god that is supposed to be all-knowing, all-powerful, and completely good. I will not discuss the arguments specifically directed at a Judaeo-Christian god here.

It is often said that Hume's arguments are criticisms of arguments from analogy to the existence of a god. That is true of some of them. But he also intends to criticise a priori arguments by using analogy and the beliefs of various peoples. Hume means to undermine the intuitions that seem to make only one possibility seem salient in a society that has been brought up with Judaeo-Christian beliefs. For instance, he points out that some people seem to have thought that the world came into existence through sex between divine beings. He argues that this is as justifiable (or as unjustifiable) a belief as a belief in the Judaeo-Christian god – after all, we know that highly organised beings structured to survive and reproduce come into existence through sex; so why should the world not have originated in some similar process? Why should a process of intelligent design have brought the universe into being? Hume lists the four sources of order that we know of in the world. They are reason, instinct, generation (i.e. sex) and vegetation (Hume 1993, 80). He means to argue that there is no rational way to choose between them on the evidence available to us.

Hume puts his central point through his mouthpiece Philo in considering arguments that an intelligent designer must have been the ultimate designer of biological organisms:

> *To say that all this order in animals and vegetables proceeds ultimately from design is begging the question: nor can that great point be ascertained otherwise than by proving a priori both that order is, from its nature, inseparably attached to thought, and that it can never, of itself, or from original unknown principles, belong to matter. (Hume 1993, 81)*

We might want to weaken the demand for proof to a demand that a high probability be shown a priori to attach itself to thought as a principle of design, but the central point is correct.

It is worth remembering here the fact that Aristotle saw no need to postulate an intelligent designer for the living beings in the world. Instead, he thought the principle of order was already built into the various biological organisms and into the celestial spheres whose order could be extrapolated into the past as far as we want. This gives us another possibility to add to the ones Hume lists in detail. Hume is aware that perhaps the fundamental order in the universe goes back to infinity, or perhaps it is just already there when the universe begins – after all, explanations have to end somewhere. Why should they not end with an order already in place? After all, as he points out, a divine mind would also have to have some sort of order in it.

Chapter 8

I have mentioned several possibilities discussed by Hume's mouthpiece, Philo. Hume attributes some of them to various peoples, but it is not necessary to attribute them to any peoples. Hume could have spun them from his own brain. The point is that they are possibilities grounded in what we see in the world extrapolated to the creation of the world. They are intended to break down a prejudice generated in our minds through exposure to the Judaeo-Christian story. One particularly striking example which illustrates how instinct can produce order is the infinite spider. As Hume puts it through his mouthpiece Philo:

> *The Brahmins assert, that the world arose from an infinite spider, who spun this whole complicated mass from his bowels . . . Here is a species of cosmogony, which appears to us ridiculous; because a spider is a little contemptible animal, whose operations we are never likely to take for a model of the whole universe. But still here is a new species of analogy, even in our globe. And were there a planet wholly inhabited by spiders (which is very possible), this inference would appear as natural and irrefragable as that which in our planet ascribes the origin of all things to design and intelligence.* (Hume 1993, 82)

Hume's point is well brought out by this example. Having been brought up where a particular view of the world has been predominant for many centuries, we tend to think of order as being brought about by things like us. But this is far from necessary. Some much more minimally intelligent thing might bring about order in the world. I do not think that I need to go to other examples in Hume to spell out his line of argument further.

Now it might be thought that since we know from modern Biology that generation, instinct, and vegetation all have arisen by mutation and natural selection, that these are not good examples of processes by which an original order of the universe could come about. However, something Hume points out can be used to make an important point here. He says that '[J]udging by our limited and imperfect experience, generation has some privileges above reason. For we see every day the latter arise from the former, never the former from the latter' (Hume 1993, 81). On the basis of this, we could argue that some sexual process is more likely to have brought about the universe than an intelligent designer. We can add, given what we know today from Biology, that we see generation and intelligent animals gradually arise from laws of nature that show no obvious glimmer of intelligence – chemical mutations and natural selection do the job.

Modern Cosmology

Before we proceed to consider some further arguments, it is worth discussing the consensus position in modern cosmology. Based on the evidence available, the universe we know is the result of a colossal explosion billions of years ago called the big bang. The laws of nature as we know them, and the basic materials from which our universe is made, originated a short time after the big bang. We do not know what the laws were at the very moment of the universe's creation. We do not know if there were preceding states before the big bang. One possibility is that everything, including time, began with the big bang. Another is that there were preceding universes or states of the universe before the big bang. We also are unsure whether there are other universes.

Modern Arguments for an Intelligent Designer: Swinburne's Arguments

One influential line of argument for a kind of theism has been presented by Richard Swinburne. I will discuss two of his arguments. The first is based on the very existence of laws of nature throughout the universe and a limited and small number of basic materials throughout space and time. Swinburne thinks that it is very surprising that there should be such laws and a small number of basic materials everywhere and everywhen. He thinks that this requires an explanation. He presents a probabilistic argument that a single designer god is the best explanation available.

A second related argument, often called the fine-tuning argument, relies on the (disputed) claim by some physicists that fundamental constants in the universe are such that even the slightest variation in them would mean that the universe as we know it could not exist, and no life-supporting universe could exist. Swinburne again thinks that it is very surprising that this supposed fact should be the case. He claims that it requires an explanation. He presents a probabilistic argument that a single designer god is the best explanation available.

Before I turn to a more detailed discussion of his arguments, let me fill in some background. A number of Hume's criticisms of arguments for a designer god were based on the view that only something analogous to our experience of causes could be justified as an explanation of the universe or of parts of it. But much modern science seems to not fit this pattern. The strangest things that do not fit our experience seem to be warranted by modern science. For instance, many features of gravity are explained in modern Physics by the curvature of space. The predictions such theories make are tested and found to be correct to a remarkable degree. This is taken to be a warrant for them. Again, the particles postulated by much of modern Physics are incredibly weird. Take the Higgs boson. It is the particle that supplies mass to other particles. Yet everything we perceive in our everyday life has mass. If we were to extrapolate by analogy, we would immediately dismiss the Higgs boson. Nevertheless, a series of remarkably exact experiments show that the Higgs exists. Science requires not merely analogical reasoning, but also inferences to the best explanation. Swinburne is aware of this and uses it in his arguments.

Swinburne's uses Bayes' Theorem, a theorem in probability, to spell out his arguments in detail. We do not need to go into those details here. Basically, what Swinburne argues is that the probability of an immaterial intelligent designer of the universe is much higher given facts like laws which operate throughout space and time, the same small number of particles everywhere, and fine-tuning. Swinburne argues that this being needs to be immaterial to explain the features of the material world – a material being would lead to a regress of explanation. He also wants to argue that material explanation comes to an end, and that an explanation in terms of persons needs to explain material explanation. Contrary to Hume, the fact the that designer is supposed to be a non-material intelligent being who explains key features of the universe is irrelevant to the plausibility of the hypothesis that such a being exists; for, after all, Physics postulates the strangest things in its explanations.

Now we can see straight away that although Swinburne is right to claim that we do not need to postulate analogous causes, he is wrong to say that analogy is not relevant. Why could a material or even immaterial cause not be more like Hume's spider? Or like a vegetable? Why does it need to be an incredibly intelligent designer? Swinburne has restricted the possible explanations to the only one he wants to justify. But, as Hume told us, there are a number of possibilities that might explain key features of the universe like those that Swinburne describes. For instance, perhaps the same laws and fundamental particles are everywhere and everywhen because the spider-like designer brought the same materials into being and keeps them working in the same way. Perhaps it needs fine-tuning to keep its system in place.

Further, why do we need an immaterial cause at all? Perhaps the beginning of the big bang is the beginning of everything. After all, explanations have to come to an end somewhere. Swinburne seems to be putting the result he wants to arrive at into his explanation.

All of this means that Swinburne's use of probability is not justified. There are too many possibilities to consider. Swinburne would need to consider the probability of his favoured explanation by comparison to the other possibilities, in particular the possibility of a relatively dumb designer being and the possibility that the explanation comes to an end with the beginning of the big bang. When we do this, it is very hard to see that any particular conclusion is justified.

Mackie's Criticisms of Swinburne's Arguments

John Mackie presents some criticisms of Swinburne's arguments and of similar arguments. I will only consider two important criticisms here. The first criticism is that once Darwinian explanations have been provided for the existence of beings which are highly adapted for survival and reproduction, there is nothing that indicates the laws or materials in the universe are end-directed. There is no reciprocal adjustment of parts which indicates purposiveness. I might add here that there is no need even for a dumb designer of the universe, such as the infinite spider.

Mackie's second important criticism is more subtle. It is that the argument from laws fails because Swinburne has to use induction to arrive at the first premise of his argument. The first premise is that the same laws and basic materials operate throughout the universe. To arrive at this from the very small sample of the universe that physicists have tested, Swinburne needs to believe that it is reasonable to extrapolate inductively whether a god exists or not. However, if he does this, he cannot also say that it is surprising that the same laws and basic materials should be found everywhere. He cannot reasonably add as a second premise the claim that such order is very unlikely unless there is a divine designer (Mackie 1982, 147–8).

Swinburne has replied in detail to various of Mackie's arguments. However, he seems to miss the point of Mackie's second important criticism (Swinburne 1991, 298–99).

I will add here an argument put by my former student Toby Freeman. The universe originated from something very small in the big bang. The laws and materials as we know them originated very soon afterwards. Given these facts, it is not surprising that the same laws and materials exist everywhere and everywhen. There would be no reason for the laws and basic materials to change over time. Had the universe always been there it might be thought to be surprising. After all, it is very large. We might think, why should the laws and basic materials be the same throughout this enormous expanse? But, on the best evidence available, it has not always been there.

Conclusion

Both ancient and modern design arguments for the existence of a god fail. The reasons the ancients had for believing in a god have been shown to be unfounded by the rise of modern science. Hume also showed that there were many possibilities to explain various features of the world, including various dumb designers. Swinburne has failed to provide a convincing design argument for the existence of a god. We have no reason to add gods to our list of kinds of being.

Further Readings

David Hume's *Dialogues Concerning Natural Religion* is the classic work in the area. The best edition available currently is Hume (1993). Part VII is the crucial part for our purposes. O'Connor (2001) is a very useful introduction to the key issues I consider here.

Mackie (1982) contains some of the most subtle and complex discussion of arguments for a designer since Hume. Chapter 8 contains a good discussion of Hume and of Swinburne's argument. Richard Swinburne includes an important argument for a designer and some subtle comments on Hume and other matters. The use of Bayes's theorem in his arguments is spelt out in detail. I think the revised first edition (Swinburne 1991) is better than later editions. The revised first edition contains a detailed reply to Mackie. Chapter 8 is the key chapter.

Grünbaum (2004) criticises a range of arguments for the existence of a god, including design arguments. Swinburne and Grünbaum continued the debate in a range of articles in the same journal. My 'Aristotle, Hume, and the Sphex Wasp at the Beginning of the Universe' puts the argument that if a designer of the universe is needed, a dumb designer fits what we know better than a highly intelligent designer. The full draft of that paper is available on my Academia.edu website. I also refer there to work by cosmologists who argue that the key premise of the fine-tuning argument is simply false. There could be interesting and stable universes without the fundamental constants in our universe.

CHAPTER 9

The Laws of Logic

There have long been debates about some fundamental laws of logic. If they are true, why are they true? While Aristotle alludes to such laws in his logical works, the full statement and defence of them is in Book Gamma of his *Metaphysics*, which starts with the statement I have quoted before that 'there is a science of being as being'. Aristotle treats two fundamental laws of logic as primarily metaphysical truths in the science of being. They are the law of non-contradiction and the law of excluded middle.

Let's start by stating his primary version of the law of non-contradiction. It is that 'the same thing cannot at the same time belong and also not belong to the same thing and in the same respect' (Aristotle 2016, 53; 1005b 18–21). In Book Kappa, it is stated that 'the same thing cannot at the same time be and not be, or admit of any other opposites in this way' (Aristotle 2016, 181; 1061b 35–1062a). (Some scholars argue that Kappa is not by Aristotle, but even they accept that it presents Aristotle's views.) Aristotle goes on to present a psychological form of the law, which is that no one can suppose the same thing to be and not be at the same time and in the same respect, and a logical form which is that opposite assertions are not simultaneously true. However, it is clear that he does not regard these as the primary version of the law. Rather, he thinks that their truth is dependent

129

on the truth of the primary version. I will only be discussing the primary version here. While the statement of the law in Kappa is slightly different, I will take it that it is a clearer version of the same law.

It should be noted that so far, Aristotle has not clearly distinguished the law of excluded middle from the law of non-contradiction. His initial statement in Gamma, for instance, could be taken to cover both non-contradiction and excluded middle. His initial statement rules out the possibility of a thing which manifests opposites at the same time in the same respect. In any case, he later states the law of excluded middle explicitly about contradictories and adds an important explanation. The law is that

> *neither is it possible for there to be anything in the middle between contradictories, but it is necessary either to affirm or to deny one thing, whatever it may be, of one thing. This will be clear if we define what truth is and what falsehood is. For to say of what is that it is not, or of what is not that it is, is false, whereas to say of what is that it is, or of what is not that it is not, is true. So he who says of anything that it is, or that it is not, will either say what is true or what is false. (Aristotle 2016, 65–66; 1011b 23–28)*

Aristotle is not making an epistemological point about uncertainty. He is directly tying the law of excluded middle to the existence or non-existence of a definite truth-maker, which makes affirmations false or true. He is saying that we can never truly affirm that there is something which is true between contradictories. For instance, Socrates must be either alive or not alive. He cannot be in some state which is between being alive and not being alive. A thing must either be a cloud or not a cloud. It cannot be neither. Aristotle also means to apply this law to regions. An area near the edge of a cloud must be either a cloud or not a cloud.

It should also be noted that Aristotle's initial statement of the law of non-contradiction rules out the possibility of a thing manifesting contrary and not merely contradictory properties at the same time. Let me spell out the standard account of contraries and contradictories before I continue. The account emanates from Aristotle's work. According to this account, two contrary statements can simultaneously be false, but they cannot both be true. Consider, for example, a plastic table. The statements 'the table is coloured blue all over' and 'the table is coloured green all over' are contraries. They apparently cannot both be true, but they can both be false, for instance, if the table is coloured red all over. We can see why Aristotle admits that there can sometimes be intermediate cases between contraries. For example, there can be a colour which is properly described as between blue and green – a blue/green. However, we will see that there is good reason to doubt the general claim that contraries cannot both be true. Turn now to contradictories. Aristotle holds that one or the other of two contradictory statements must be true. The table is blue all over and the table is not blue all over are such that, if the table exists, one or the other of them must be true. We will see that there is good reason to doubt that two contradictory statements simultaneously cannot both be true, at least in the case of the phenomenology of perception.

A common view in more recent literature is that the law of non-contradiction and the law of excluded middle are conceptual or linguistic truths, not metaphysical truths. On this account, this is why they have been built into the standard version of modern logic, which was the result of developments in modern logic pioneered by Gottlob Frege in the nineteenth century, and Bertrand Russell in the twentieth century. By contrast, Aristotle thinks they are truths about the world that are universal. His view is that it is in virtue of them being true about the world that they are also conceptual or linguistic truths. He also holds that they are necessary truths. One important sense in which he thinks that they are necessary is that we cannot coherently describe a world in which they are false.

To understand why Aristotle stresses that these laws are primarily about the world, it is important to state that these laws cannot be undermined through the problematic use of language. Ambiguity does not undermine these laws. For instance, the statement 'it is raining' and the statement 'it is not raining' are not contradictory statements unless we specify that we are talking about the exact same place and time. Neither are 'the bank is ahead of us' and 'the bank is not ahead of us' contradictory if the first statement refers to a savings bank and the second statement refers to a river bank. Further, linguistic vagueness does not undermine these laws. 'It is raining' is vague as to how many raindrops are involved and as to their size, so it might be thought that it could be raining and not raining if just a few small drops are involved. But that would not be a contradiction in the world and hence does not pose problems for Aristotle's two laws. Rather, it would be an indication that we need to be more precise in our language to correctly describe the world.

Plato's and Aristotle's Arguments for the Laws

Aristotle does not present detailed arguments for these laws in his works on logic. He presents arguments for them in the course of his metaphysical discussion in *Metaphysics Gamma*. Aristotle starts by telling us that he cannot directly argue for the truth of these laws as all our reasoning assumes that they are true. Nevertheless, he presents a number of arguments for these laws, which rely on whether it is possible to deny these laws coherently. Some of Aristotle's arguments resemble the argument against Cratylus that Plato presented in the *Theaetetus*, which I have briefly discussed in chapter 1. Protagoras is also a target of Plato's critique in the *Theaetetus*. I will assume that Aristotle's key arguments are aimed at Cratylus and Protagoras.

Following Plato, Aristotle is concerned about two theses:

First, Protagoras's relativistic denial of the existence of (intrinsic) essential properties (the denial that there is what it is to be something). Aristotle takes the crucial bit of Protagoras's relativism to be that something only has properties in relation to a perceiver. This means that Protagoras would allow non-contradiction to be false as, at the same time, one perceiver could truly perceive X to have property R and another perceiver truly perceive it to have property not-R.

Second, Cratylus's claim that everything is changing in every respect all of the time. This too denies (intrinsic) essential properties, for in flux world there is nothing that is what it is to be something. (For Aristotle, there would not even be intrinsic essential properties at a point in time, for he thinks points in time are mathematical fictions.)

For Aristotle, as for Plato, the connection between the two theses is that both deny the existence of (intrinsic) essential properties.

Against Aristotle puts various claims, such as: (a) If something is being destroyed, that thing must be in the process of destruction and still exist, and if something is coming to be, it must be coming to be out of something definite, and this cannot go on to infinity (Aristotle 2016, 62; 1010a 20). (b) Cratylus has failed to distinguish quantitative from qualitative change – change in quantity might be continuous, but that doesn't mean that change in quality is – something can continue to be the same kind of thing while constantly changing in quantity. We are acquainted with things through their kind (Aristotle 2016, 85; 1010a 23–25). (c) That the thesis is incoherent because 'it is necessary that that what is changes, since change is from something into something' (Aristotle 2016, 68; 1012b 27–29). I take it that the argument is that there cannot be change if everything is changing in every respect all the time, as there is no state of definite being to change out of or into.

CHAPTER 9

All of this seems weak as a critique of a more modest thesis than that of Cratylus. Why not allow that things are stable in certain respects, but not in others? Then that allows us to identify a thing which is changing. But Aristotle will say that it's only *in that respect* that it's changing, and *in that respect* it must be something to change into something else – otherwise, we have replacement not change. Something new appears from nowhere. If we have replacement, non-contradiction isn't threatened. So, no argument from change can undermine the principle of non-contradiction. (Aristotle would then presumably try to rule out replacement by using the principle that nothing comes from nothing, which he takes to be obviously true – the replacement thesis denies this principle).

But what underlies Aristotle's critique of Cratylus that links these arguments to non-contradiction? As I understand Gamma, Aristotle thinks that there are four central claims that are true of being, the first three of which are either equivalent to or almost equivalent to the principle of non-contradiction in its primary form. This is why the science of being qua being, which Aristotle indicates at the beginning of Gamma is the central subject of discussion in Gamma, deals with both the fundamental principles of demonstration and the most general and necessary features of being. Both are dependent on metaphysical necessities. The first three claims seem to sit behind much of the later part of Gamma; the fourth claim is defended elsewhere. As Aristotle sees it, the first three claims are denied by Cratylus, and the fourth is implicitly denied by Cratylus and explicitly denied by Protagoras. These claims are:

A) For there to be being (there to be anything that is), there must (synchronically) be a what it is to be of anything that is.
B) For there to be being (there to be anything that is), there must (diachronically) be a what it was to be of any thing that is.

C) The what it is to be and what it was to be of a thing is an essence, or is composed out of things that have essences. An essence is a feature that a thing must have to be that thing. The continuing presence of the essences explains the continuity of diachronic continuants. In the case of non-essential necessary properties, they arise out of essences. The same is true of accidental properties. For example, it might be said that my cat Pushkin has a catty essence which is what it is to be her. This catty essence explains why the embryo Pushkin and the adult Pushkin are the same thing. Finally, this catty essence explains what Pushkin characteristically does – it is what most explains her characteristic causal powers/capacities.
D) Truth in statements corresponds to a truth-maker. A truth-maker is something existing entirely independently of the perceiver in a relation that corresponds to a descriptive sentence (e.g. 'the cat is on the mat' is true if and only if the cat in the world is on the mat in the world, whether anyone perceives this fact or not).

CRITICISMS OF ARISTOTLE

The key issue in these arguments is whether there can be a world which is indeterminate that we can describe coherently. To be more precise, it is whether there can be a world which is indeterminate in some respects. At times, Aristotle wants to turn the claim that the world is indeterminate in some respects into the broader claim that the world is wholly indeterminate, a claim which would make talk about the world incoherent. But it is by no means obvious that the claim that the world is indeterminate in some respects justifies the claim that the world is wholly indeterminate. Let us try to focus on some examples.

Take the edges of objects. To everyday appearance, objects seem to have sharp edges. Suppose I touch my table with a finger. It is pretty clear, by and large, that most of my finger is separate from the table. Similarly, most of the table is separate from my finger. Non-contradiction and excluded middle seem to be true of many remarks about my finger. For instance, the back part of my finger is made of skin. The statement the back part of my finger is not made of skin is false. Non-contradiction seems to be true in this case. It also seems to be true of many remarks about the table. For instance, that the vast majority of the table is made of plastic. The statement the vast majority of the table is not made of plastic is false. But what about the small region in which my finger is touching the table? Indeed, what about where my finger is touching the table? Is it so clear that there is not a region in which finger and table intermingle? What do we say about this region? A cloud and the surrounding air is perhaps a clearer example. Is there a precise place where the cloud ceases and the surrounding air begins? Or is there a small area in which the two intermingle? The central point here, of course, is not about what we say but about what is there in the world. Must it be the case that there is a clear and sharp separation between one thing and another in the world?

Consider what we might say if there is no clear and sharp separation between one thing and another in the world, no matter how much we refine our definitions. Do we say that the area where cloud and cold air merge is both cloud and not cloud? If we say that, we seem to be denying non-contradiction. Alternatively, we might say that this is an intermediate case, in which we seem to be denying the law of excluded middle, though not precisely as the law has been stated by Aristotle.

Again, let us take changes over time. Suppose Socrates is dying. Is there some precise point or very small region in time at which Socrates is dead? It is hard to see that there is, even if we refine our definitions with the best medical knowledge possible. If there is not a precise point or region in time, do we say that non-contradiction is wrong or that the excluded middle is wrong? Whether they are wrong or not, are they necessary truths?

Now consider changes over evolutionary time. Consider the ancestors of humans. It is hard to see that there is a sharp cutoff point between ancestral apes and humans. Human evolutionary ancestors will include intermediate cases. Aristotle assumed, at least by and large, that species are fixed. But we learn from evolution that this is not the case.

I will argue here that it is the excluded middle that may be wrong, and that it is not a necessary truth. But to state my argument, I need to engage in a refinement of logical claims. When we say that something is indeterminate between two states, we are, in fact, talking about contraries, not contradictories. Aristotle admits that there can be intermediate states between some contraries but does not seem to grasp the implications of this fact. As I said earlier, when you look at his statement of non-contradiction, he does not sharply distinguish between contradictories and contraries.

To say that Socrates is in an intermediate state between being alive and dead is not simply to say that he is alive and not alive. The things in the world that are not alive include the sun, rocks and many other things. We are not saying that Socrates is among those things, at least when Socrates is in the process of dying. Even if Socrates is recently dead, he is a dead human body, a specific kind of thing. Over time, he may become dust and parts of his dead body may become part of a rock. But that is not what we are considering. We are considering the time when he is in an intermediate state between being a living human and a very recently dead human.

A standard way in which we infer conclusions means that we convert denials of excluded middle about some contraries to denials of non-contradiction about those contraries. If Socrates is in an intermediate state between being a living human and being a dead human, we are inclined to think that this implies that Socrates is both alive and not alive. But, as I pointed out, to say that Socrates is not alive is a vague description that covers

Chapter 9

Socrates possibly being a rock, dirt and many other things. This is not what we are saying when we say that Socrates is in an intermediate state between being a living human and not being a living human. It does not follow that Socrates is simply not alive when we say that he is in this intermediate state.

We can say the same sort of thing about cases in which something is intermediate in space. To say that something is between a cloud and cold air is not to say that it is both a cloud and not a cloud. Being not a cloud includes very many other things.

Again, when we say that what is now a fossil was intermediate between a human and a non-human ape, we are not saying that it was simply not a human.

A key point here is that our linguistic habits are misleading. We quickly convert contraries into contradictories, but we need not do so in all cases. Let us turn back to Aristotle. Aristotle's initial statement of non-contradiction covers both contraries and contradictories. He wants to push those who deny the excluded middle in any form into denying non-contradiction. But this only follows if we accept our linguistic habits. We can introduce two types of negation to make the point clearer. The negation involved in an intermediate state will be designated by a small n, and the negation involved in a state that is not intermediate will be designated by a big N. So, an intermediate state is designated by (a) Socrates is alive and n alive. A contradictory state is indicated by (b) Socrates is alive and N alive. As Aristotle says, it is difficult to state precisely what is involved in b. If we assert it, do we mean that Socrates is alive, or do we mean that Socrates is alive and one of the things that are definitely N alive? By contrast, what is involved in a is easily comprehensible.

We can apply the same treatment to the spatial problem I mentioned above. When we say that an area is both cloud and the cloudless surrounding cold air, we are not saying that it is cloud and N cloud; rather, we are saying it is cloud and n cloud. If we are saying that an area in space is both cloud and n cloud, we are not saying that an area is both a cloud and any of the other things in the world.

There is no joy for the Protagorean relativist in what I have said. Nevertheless, a Heraclitean can take some comfort in it. For some pretty narrow spatial areas and some pretty narrow temporal regions, it is reasonable to say that some contrary states may be true of them. This does not mean that everything is always changing in every respect all of the time, as Cratylus is said to have asserted – that would still be incoherent.

I have argued in detail that excluded middle about contraries is not a necessary truth. Further, as far as I can tell, excluded middle about contraries is false. However, I have not produced a decisive argument that it is false, only that there is good reason to think that Aristotle is wrong. Perhaps more precise definitions can be given in all cases, which will show that excluded middle is true. However, I can see no evidence that that is the case.

THE SORITES PARADOX AND EXCLUDED MIDDLE

An important issue is whether there must be a clear dividing line between the intermediate states that I have described above and the states that are not intermediate. Does there have to be a clear dividing line between Socrates being alive/n alive, and Socrates being alive, for instance? To understand the problem, a good starting point is the so-called sorites paradox. In its original Greek formulation, it involves a heap. Suppose there is a heap of wheat seeds. Take one seed away from a heap and what is left is clearly a heap. Suppose we now formulate the principle that whenever we take away a seed from a heap, we are always left with a heap. We can see that this will quickly lead us to some dubious cases. As we keep taking away the seeds, it will turn out that even one seed is a heap. Now, heap is a rather ill-defined concept. So, the problem can be made to go away if we stipulate a precise definition of a heap in which a precise number of seeds of a particular size and weight constitutes a heap. Arguably, there is no blurriness in the world in the case of heaps. However, we can apply the same line of argument to being alive. Suppose Socrates is alive but very ill. Take the next one ten-thousandth of a second, and the one after it. We reasonably formulate the principle that someone who is alive is also going to be alive a ten-thousandth of a second later. This will lead via a series of steps to the conclusion that someone who is alive/n alive is also alive. It will eventually even lead to the conclusion that someone who is dead is alive/n alive.

How can we escape the sorites paradox in such cases? One suggestion is that it is an epistemic paradox, that we cannot tell when or where one thing begins and another ends. But this seems implausible. If we accept my analysis of being alive/n alive and other cases, we can see that there is no good reason to assume that there must be a sharp cutoff in the world between one thing and another, and one state and another. We can also see that there need not be a sharp cutoff point between intermediate states and states that are not intermediate. On one account, the ancient Greek philosopher Chryssipus of Soli thought that there were no such sharp cutoff points, and that no precise statement could capture such cases. In response to a series of questions posed by an interlocutor, he recommended that we fall silent about dubious cases. In such cases, no proposition is warranted. Of course, there are also clear cases. In such cases, Chryssipus thought we should give an answer. For instance, Socrates is alive. This is his solution to the sorites paradox. If Chryssipus is right, then there are blurry cases in the world about which we should fall silent, as no statement will truly capture what is there in the world. However, as I have said above, I think in such cases we can produce statements that are true and violate the excluded middle. For instance, Socrates is both alive and n alive.

One possible response to the arguments I have presented so far is that I have not been dealing with true contraries. True contraries are incompatible. They cannot be present together. That is what it is to be a contrary. A problem with this response is that it may be that there are no true contraries in the world. Perhaps Aristotle and others are just wrong in thinking that there are true contraries because, for a tiny stretch of time and for a tiny stretch of space, beings in the world meld into one another.

Contradictions in Phenomenology

One line of argument in recent literature on the laws of logic is that while non-contradiction is perhaps true of the world, it is not true of phenomenology, of our perception of aspects of the world. On this account, to describe our phenomenology correctly, we must describe some objects in it as having inconsistent properties. Non-contradiction is not only not necessarily true of our phenomenology but clearly false. A further conclusion which some logicians have drawn from the phenomenological examples is that this shows that non-contradiction is not a necessary truth, even if it is a truth.

Consider the image below of a so-called 'three-dimensional combination triangle' invented by Chris Mortensen and his students. Focus on the white surface at the bottom of the triangle, which starts on the underneath left side of the triangle. It is obvious that as we move our attention from the left to the right and then up the right side of the triangle that the white surface is both on the outer edge of the triangle and on the inner edge of the triangle. That violates both excluded middle and non-contradiction. The light grey surface on the left is both on the outer edge of the triangle and not on the outer part of the triangle as we move towards the left part of it. Pictures that produce a similar inconsistent phenomenology abound in the work of Escher and others. So, this picture is not an isolated exception (figure 9.1).

Now, I know of nothing in the world that is like our inconsistent representation. As far as I can tell, nothing in our world violates non-contradiction. These apparent things are only ways in which we mentally represent diagrams we perceive in our world. Nevertheless, the phenomenology raises an interesting question.

CHAPTER 9

Figure 9.1 An Inconsistent Image Source: Created by the author

Could such things exist in the real world? Does the phenomenology show that the law of non-contradiction is not a necessary truth about the world, even if it is a truth about the world? It is difficult to answer this question. If such things existed, we would not know how to negotiate them. Suppose such a thing existed. Suppose now we were trying to move along the lower white surface to go to the inside right surface of the vertex in the triangle. We would seem to end up going to something that is both the outside surface and not the outside surface of the triangle. But perhaps all this would mean is that a merely outside surface does not exist in that place. There seems to be no reason to say that contradictions cannot exist in reality as opposed to just saying that, in fact, they do not exist. Note that in the case of the triangle and similar cases, we are not dealing with contraries.

ESSENCES REVISITED

How does the account I have produced sit with my defence of essences in an earlier chapter? Is it not the case that the characteristic powers or capacities of such things are not determinately one thing or another if they have contrary essences during the same time interval? If something is transitional between non-human ape and human, what is its essence? If Socrates is alive/n alive, what is his essence during that very small period of time? What are his characteristic powers or capacities?

Different cases require different answers. The transitional being, which is not yet fully human, will have an essence, but it will not fit into a neat biological category. It will have its own characteristic powers and capacities. Essences are not universals, as we have seen in an earlier chapter. The Socrates case and similar cases pose a tougher problem. It is unclear whether at this tiny transitional time between two essences, it has an essence which is clearly defined. Similar comments can be made about the spatial cases. Perhaps then, some things at some times do not have a clear essence. The world is just blurry in such cases. Note, however, that it is not indefinitely blurry. It is blurry between two pretty clear states. This means that I will have to modify my remarks about essences in an earlier chapter. Some things in transitional states do not have a definite essence and definite causal powers, even though they are not completely indefinite. Heracliteanism seems to be true of such cases.

Let me note, however, that as I said above, I have not produced a decisive argument that there are such transitional cases. I have only shown that there could be such cases. Excluded middle about contraries is not a necessary truth. However, perhaps it is a truth.

Conclusion

We have seen that there are good reasons to deny excluded middle about contraries. It is not a necessary truth and may well be false. If it is false, we will have to limit the claims I made about essences and causal powers in earlier chapters. For some transitional cases in the world, there may be no definite essences. Nevertheless, the world is not indefinitely blurry in such cases. It is blurry between certain alternative states. What about excluded middle about contradictories? Does the falsity of excluded middle about contraries imply the falsity of excluded middle about contradictories? As excluded middle about contradictories is different from excluded middle about contraries, it is not clear that we can conclude that excluded middle about contradictories is false if excluded middle about contraries is false. Some logicians have produced formal systems in which the denial of excluded middle can be converted into the denial of non-contradiction. Whether those formal systems really reflect what is happening in the world is unclear. I will leave this problem to the reader to further consider.

We have also seen that non-contradiction is not true of the phenomenology of inconsistent images. This means that although non-contradiction seems to be true about the world, it is not a necessary truth about the world. Perhaps the reader can think of examples in the world where non-contradiction is false.

FURTHER READINGS

The classic defence of non-contradiction and excluded middle is Book Gamma of Aristotle's *Metaphysics*. Politis (2004) contains several excellent chapters on Aristotle's arguments for non-contradiction and excluded middle. He argues for a different conclusion from mine. Graham Priest has criticised Aristotle's defence of non-contradiction in detail in Priest (1998). The paper is available on Priest's website. Chryssipus's arguments are discussed in detail in Bobzien (2002). The draft of the paper is available on Suzanne Bobzien's Academia.edu website. Chris Mortensen has presented a range of examples of inconsistent figures in Mortensen (2022). His much more technical discussion of inconsistent figures and of the possibility of real inconsistent objects is in Mortensen (2010). That book also contains some non-technical discussion of inconsistent figures.

Epilogue

We have seen that approaching Metaphysics as the science of being as being, and starting with Aristotle's arguments, is an illuminating way to discuss the various kinds of being and the various arguments. Many of Aristotle's key theses when modernised are very plausible. The notions of substance, essence and attribute are useful for understanding things and how they behave. The notion of capacity, disposition, or power allows us to understand much of modern scientific thought. Nevertheless, some of Aristotle's views cannot be accepted today. Aristotle's rejection of external relations and his theory of space are implausible, despite some modern attempts to defend them. Aristotle's view that gods are needed to explain various features of the world has been superseded by advancements in science. Aristotle is to be praised for presenting the fundamental laws of logic as part of the science of being as being rather than some conceptual laws. By seeing them as laws which apply to the world, we can understand some problems with them. As I have argued, the law of excluded middle may well be false. Further, non-contradiction is false about phenomenology.

Some topics which could be pursued through Aristotle's arguments are the nature of time, the nature of numbers, the nature of imaginary and fictional objects.

Epilogue

Aristotle's discussion of time is rather opaque. He thinks of time as some relation between measurements, but much of the rest of his account is unclear. In the sixth century, John Philoponus interpreted Aristotle and presented a much more luminous account of time based on ironing out unclarities in Aristotle's account. I have discussed that account briefly elsewhere (Couvalis 2017). Can that account be modernised? The Theories of Special and General Relativity have transformed our understanding of time. It would be a worthwhile task to work out the details of an Aristotelian account that takes account of Relativity. Perhaps such an account would be viable.

Aristotle's discussion of numbers and his account of geometry are of considerable interest. He presents an abstractionist theory of numbers. The predominant Frege/Russell view of numbers was initiated by Frege through a rejection of abstractionism. That view plausibly replaces numbers with logical devices but is deficient as an account of magnitude numbers – numbers which describe quantities of various things, such as mass. It is also psychologically implausible as an account of our ideas of numbers, even where a logically equivalent account of numbers can be produced. Mendell (2004) gives a cogent account of Aristotle's view. Can abstractionism be rescued from Fregean criticisms? It would be an interesting exercise to try to defend it against such criticisms. We have seen that there are reasons for accepting Aristotle's abstractionist view of geometry when it is added to an account of idealisation. Perhaps the same can be done with Aristotle's account of numbers.

A related issue to the issue of giving a plausible account of numbers is the issue of giving a plausible account of intentional objects, such as mathematical objects and fictional objects. We talk as if they exist in some sense. Meinong and his followers have argued that we can give an account of the sense in which they exist without existing in the real world (Reicher 2022). Aristotle rejected the existence of such objects and produced an interesting account of intentionality. Can that account be modernised? Arguably, it can be. There has been an interesting attempt to modernise it (Caston 1998). Perhaps that can be expanded.

There are other issues that can perhaps be tackled by starting from an Aristotelian standpoint. Aristotle's biological works suggest that he treats biological substances as processes rather than just as things. This is an interesting line of thought which could be expanded by merging with recent work in process philosophy (Seibt 2022). Unlike Plato's *Republic*, Aristotle's *Politics* arguably contains the germ of a Metaphysics of society which is not implicitly authoritarian. And so on.

REFERENCES

Aquinas. 1937. *On Being and Essence.* Translated by George Leckie. New York: Appleton-Century-Crofts.
Aristotle. 1928. *Metaphysics.* Translated by W.D. Ross. 2nd ed. Oxford: Oxford University Press.
Aristotle. 1955. "On Coming-To-Be and Passing Away". Translated by E.S. Foster, 162–329. In *Aristotle III.* London: Heinemann. 1955
Aristotle. 1963. *Categories and De Interpretatione.* Translated by J.L. Ackrill. Oxford: Oxford University Press.
Aristotle. 1976. *Metaphysics M and N.* Translated by Julia Annas. Oxford: Oxford University Press.
Aristotle. 1996. *Physics.* Translated by Robin Waterfield. Introduction by David Bostock. Oxford: Oxford University Press.
Aristotle. 2016. *Metaphysics.* Translated by C.D.C. Reeve. Indianapolis: Hackett Publishing Company.
Armstrong, David. 1989. *Universals, an Opinionated Introduction.* Boulder: Westview Press.
Armstrong, David. 1997. *A World of States of Affairs.* Cambridge: Cambridge University Press.
Arntzenhuis, Frank. 2008. "Gunk, Topology, Measure", in *Oxford Studies in Metaphysics, volume 4*, edited by Dean Zimmerman, 225–246. Oxford: Oxford University Press.
Bobzien, Suzanne. 2002 "Chrysippus and the Epistemic Theory of Vagueness." *Proceedings of the Aristotelian Society* 102: 217–238.
Burnyeat, Myles. 1990. *The Theaetetus of Plato.* Indianapolis: Hackett Publishing Company.
Cartwright, Nancy. 1983. *How the Laws of Physics Lie.* Oxford: Oxford University Press.
Cartwright, Nancy. 1989. *Nature's Capacities and Their Measurement.* Oxford: Oxford University Press.
Cartwright, Nancy. 1999. "Aristotelian Natures and the Modern Experimental Method." In *The Dappled World*, edited by Nancy Cartwright, 77–103. Cambridge: Cambridge University Press.
Couvalis, George. 2017. "Philoponus on the Nature of Time." *Modern Greek Studies (Australia and New Zealand) Special Issue*: 27–38.

References

Caston, Victor. 1998. "Aristotle and the Problem of Intentionality". *Philosophy and Phenomenological Research* LVIII: 249–98.
Dainton, Barry. 2010. *Time and Space*, 2nd ed. Durham: Acumen.
Ellis, Brian. 2001. *Scientific Essentialism*. Cambridge: Cambridge University Press.
Grant, Edward. 1981. *Much Ado About Nothing*. Cambridge: Cambridge University Press.
Grünbaum, Adolf. 1967. *Modern Science and Zeno's Paradoxes*. Connecticut: Wesleyan University Press.
Grünbaum, Adolf. 2004. "The Poverty of Theistic Cosmology." *British Journal for the Philosophy of Science* 55: 561–614.
Heil, John. 2003. *From an Ontological Point of View*. Oxford: Oxford University Press.
Hume, David. 1993. *Dialogues and Natural History of Religion*. Oxford: Oxford University Press.
Hume, David. 2007. *A Treatise of Human Nature, Volume 1*. Edited by David Fate Norton and Mary Norton. Oxford: Oxford University Press.
Kant, Immanuel. 1968. "Concerning the Ultimate Foundation of the Differentiation of Regions in Space. In *Kant, Selected Pre-Critical Writings*. Translated by G.B. Kerferd and D.E. Walford, with P.G. Lucas, 36–44. Manchester: Manchester University Press.
Kant, Immanuel. 1996. *Critique of Pure Reason*. Translated by Werner Pluhar. Introduction by Patricia Kitcher. Indianapolis: Bloomington.
Kenny, Anthony. 2002. *Aquinas on Being*. Oxford: Oxford University Press.
Le Roi, Armand. 2014. *The Lagoon*. London: Bloomsbury Circus.
Leibniz, Gottfried. 1998. "Monadology." In *G.W. Leibniz Philosophical Texts*, Translated by R.S. Woolhouse and Richard Francks, 267–284. Oxford: Oxford University Press.
Loux, Michael. 2013. "Aristotle on Universals." In *A Companion to Aristotle*, edited by Georgios Anagnostopoulos, 186–196. Chichester: Wiley-Blackwell.
Lowe, E. J. 1995. *Routledge Philosophy Guidebook to Locke on Human Understanding*. London: Routledge.
Mackie, John. 1982. *The Miracle of Theism*. Oxford: Oxford University Press.
Marmodoro, Anna. 2014. *Aristotle on Perceiving Objects*. Oxford: Oxford University Press.
Marmodoro, Anna and Yates, David, Editors. 2016. *The Metaphysics of Relations*. Oxford: Oxford University Press.
Martin, Charles and Heil, John. 1999. "The Ontological Turn." *Midwest Studies in Philosophy* XXIII: 34–60.
Mendell, Henry. 2004. "Aristotle and Mathematics." https://plato.stanford.edu/entries/aristotle-mathematics/#7.1
Mortensen, Chris. 2010. *Inconsistent Geometry*. Studies in Logic. 27. London: College Publications.
Mortensen, Chris. 2022. *The Impossible Arises, Oscar Reutesvärd and his Contemporaries*. Indianapolis: Indiana University Press.

References

Nerlich, Graham. 1994a. *What Space-Time Explains*. Cambridge: Cambridge University Press.
Nerlich, Graham. 1994b. *The Shape of Space*, 2nd ed. Cambridge: Cambridge University Press.
Ockham, William. 1974. *Ockham's Theory of Terms, Part I of the Summa Logicae*. Translated by Michael Loux. Notre Dame: University of Notre Dame Press.
Ockham, William. 1991a. *Quodlibetal Questions, Volume 1, Quodlibets 1–4*. Translated by Alfred Freddoso and Francis Kelley. New Haven: Yale University Press.
Ockham, William. 1991b. *Quodlibetal Questions, Volume 2, Quodlibets 5–7*. Translated by Alfred Freddoso. New Haven: Yale University Press.
O'Connor, David. 2001. *Hume on Religion*. London: Routledge.
Philoponus, John. 2014. "Corollaries on Place and Void." Translated by David Furley. In *Philoponus, Corollaries on Place and Void, and Simplicius, Against Philoponus on the Eternity of the World*. London: Bloomsbury.
Plato. 1973. *Theaetetus*. Translated by John McDowell. Oxford: Oxford University Press.
Plato. 2000. *Timaeus*. Translated by Donald Zeyl. Indianapolis: Hackett.
Politis, Vassilis. 2004. *Routledge Philosophy Guidebook to Aristotle and the Metaphysics*. London: Routledge.
Priest, Graham. 1998. "To Be and Not To Be – That is the Answer. On Aristotle on the Law of Non-Contradiction." *Philosophiegeschichte und Logische Analyse* 199(1): 91–130.
Reicher, Maria. 2022. "Non-Existent Objects." https://plato.stanford.edu/entries/nonexistent-objects/.
Russell, B. 1913. "Theory of Knowledge." In *The Collected Papers of Bertrand Russell 7*, edited by Elizabeth Eames and Kenneth Blackwell, 5–178. 1984. London: Allen and Unwin.
Russell, Bertrand. 1918. "The Philosophy of Logical Atomism." In *The Collected Papers of Bertrand Russell 8*, Edited by John Slater, 157–244. 1986. London: Allen and Unwin.
Russell, Bertrand. 1926. *Our Knowledge of the External World*, Revised ed. London: Allen and Unwin.
Russell, Bertrand. 1938. *Principles of Mathematics*. New York: Norton and Company.
Russell, Bertrand. 1956. *Portraits from Memory*. New York: Simon and Schuster.
Russell, Bertrand. 1997. *The Problems of Philosophy*. Oxford: Oxford University Press.
Schiefsky, Mark. 2007. "Galen's Teleology and Functional Explanation." *Oxford Studies in Ancient Philosophy* 33: 369–400.
Seibt, Johanna. 2022. "Process Philosophy." https://plato.stanford.edu/entries/process-philosophy/.
Sklar, Lawrence. 1982. *The Philosophy of Physics*. Boulder: Westview Press.

REFERENCES

Sorabji, Richard, Editor. 1987. *Philoponus and the Rejection of Aristotelian Science.* London: Duckworth.

Sorabji, Richard. 1990. "Infinite Power Impressed: The Transformation of Aristotle's Physics and Theology." In *Aristotle Transformed: The Ancient Commentators and their Influence*, edited by Richard Sorabji, 181–198. London: Duckworth.

Strawson, Peter. 1959. *Individuals.* London: Methuen.

Strawson, Galen. 2006. "Realistic Monism." *Journal of Consciousness Studies* 13(10–11): 3–31.

Swinburne, Richard. 1991. *The Existence of God*, 2nd ed. Oxford: Oxford University Press.

Vikko, Risto and Hintikka, Jaako. 2006. "Existence and Predication from Aristotle to Frege." *Philosophy and Phenomenological Research* 73: 359–377.

Waterfield, Robin, -Translator. 2000. *The First Philosophers.* Oxford: Oxford University Press.

Xenophon. 1923. *Memorabilia and Oeconomicus.* Translated by E.C. Marchant. London: William Heinemann.

Index

abstraction and idealisation, 59–60, 63
accepted beliefs, 4
Andronicus of Rhodes, ix
Aquinas, T., 17–18
Aquinas's criticism of science of being: essence is an essence, 17–19; explanation, 17–18; Ockham's response to, 18–19
Aristotle's solutions, paradoxes, 99–103, 107, 110, 113
Aristotle's view: existence of body, 82; implausibility, 83; individual things as primary substances, 50; kinds of organisms, 119; lines, spheres and other geometrical objects, 111; non-existence of void, 82; of relations, 66; shared essences, 51; space is superfluous, 82, 85, 94, 112; species as secondary substances, 50; world is indeterminate, 135
Armstrong, D., ix, 56, 60, 71–73; view of relations, 71–73
atomism, 15

attributes: categorical properties, 56; causal powers, xiv; and disposition, 44–45; and essence, xiv; and essential properties, 34; genetic inheritance, 34; secondary kind of being, 44

beliefs are true, 3–5
biological individuals: essence, 40–43
biology, 1, 2
Bobzien, S., 144

Cantor, G., 105, 106, 113
Cartwright, N., 60
categorical properties, 56–57
causal powers of space, 57
characteristic powers and liabilities, 37, 39–40, 42–43. *See also* disposition
Clarke, S., 85, 90
concept of being, 26–30
Constable, J., 45
contingent facts, 54
Cratyleanism, 6–7
Cratylus, 5–11

critiques of science of being: Aquinas's criticism, 17–18; concept of being, 26–30; essence is an essence, 17–19; hallucination, 21–22, 25; higher-level property, 25–26; Hume's and Russell's criticism, 19–21; mathematical *vs.* fictional objects, 24–25; neutral monism, 22–24; Ockham's response to Aquinas's argument, 18–19; perceptual faculties, 23–24; property of being, 19–21; Russell's solution, 21–26

Dainton, B., 97, 113
Darwin, C., 51
denseness, 104
denumerable infinity, 106
Descartes, R., 51, 96
diachronic being, 13, 41
disposition, 54–55, 60; and attribute, 44–45

Ellis, B., ix, 56, 61
Empedocles, 118, 119
empiricism, xi, xii, 20
entities, xi–xii
episteme of being, 2
essence, xi–xiii; Aquinas arguments, xiii; and attributes, xiv; biological individuals, 40–43; causal powers/capacities, xiv; characteristic powers and liabilities, 39–40; criticisms, 43–44; and existence, 14–15, 17–19; Lockean essence, 36–38; nature of, 39–40; primary substance, 34; shared essence, 50–51; substance, xiv, 10; and substance, 35–36; things, 10
essential properties, 34
ethical beliefs, 5
everything is changing, 5–6, 133
excluded middle, xvi–xvii, 130, 131, 136–41, 143–45
existence, x, xi; being with, 3; and essences, 14–15; general idea of, 19–20; gods, xvi; Hume arguments, xiii–xiv; Kant's view, xiv; as property, xiii–xiv; propositional function, 21; Russell arguments, xiii–xiv; Russell's account of, 24; universals, xiv; of universals. *See* universals
existence of a god, 115, 120, 127, 128
existence of a plenum, 83
existence of (intrinsic) essential properties, 133
experience: Hume and Russel explanation, 25–26; Ockham's argument, 29
external objects, concept of: from experience, 20, 29–30; Ockham's argument, 29–30
external relations, xi, 66–67, 70, 72, 75, 78–79

false beliefs, 4
feature of the world, 49–50
fictional objects, 24–25

formed matter, 38–39
form of a thing, 35–36
Frege, G., 30, 31, 146

god/gods: ancient world, 116–19; Gamma Book, 1; intelligent designer, 117, 121, 125; movements in the heavens, xvi; prime mover, 117
Grant, E., 97

hallucination, 21–22, 25
Heil, J., xiii, 56, 57, 75–76, 79
Heracliteanism, xiii
Heraclitus, xiii, 5–8
Heraclitus's view of being: criticism, 7–8; everything is changing, 5–6; explanation, 5–6; nothing is anything, 7–8
Hume, D., xii, xiii, xiv, xv, 6–7, 11–14, 19–20, 58
Hume, D., modern world: generation, 122, 123; instinct, 121, 122; reason, 121; vegetation, 121, 122
Hume's and Russell's criticism of science of being: existence as propositional function, 21; experience, 25–26; hallucination, 21–22, 25; higher-level property, 25–26; idea of existence, 19–20; mathematical vs. fictional objects, 24–25; neutral monism, 22–24; non-existent things, 20; perceptual faculties, 23–24; property of being, 19–21; Russell's solution, 21–26
Hume's view of being: collections of parts, 11–12; existence and essences, 14–15; experience and its contents, 6–7; minute/minor changes, 12–14; modern Cratyleanism, 6–7; responses to, 11–15; unity and continuity, 13–14
hylomorphism, 38–40

identity, 7, 34, 37–39
immanent universals, 61, 62
immaterial form of humanity, 50
infinitesimal, 109, 110
innateness and experience, xii
internal relations, 71–73
itself through itself, 9

Kant, I., xiv, 30
kind of matter, 35–37
kinds of being, x

law of nature, 53; abstraction and idealisation, 59–60; contingent facts, 54; dispositions of things, 60; experience, 58; knowledge of essences/dispositions, 58–59; regularities and generalisation, 57–58; science of geometry, 59–60; science under certain conditions, 59
laws of being, xvi–xvii
Leibniz, G., xv, 68–70, 85–91, 93, 110

Locke, J., ix, 36–37, 51
Lockean essence, 36–38
Lowe, J., 73–75

Martin, C., 56, 57
material objects, xv–xvi
mathematical objects, 24–25
Melissus of Samos, ix
Melissus's view, 82–83
metaphysics, ix–xi, xiii, xvii; meaning, 2–3; science, 1–2
mode of being, 74
modern science and philosophy, xi
modern solutions, paradoxes: Grünbaum, Adolf, 107, 113; Russell, Bertrand, 21–26, 107, 108, 112
modern world: consensus position, 123; Darwinian account, 120, 126; Higgs boson, 124; Hume, David, 120–23; Mackie, John, 126–27; Swinburne, Richard, 123–27
monadistic view of relations, 68–69, 73–76
monistic view of relations, 69–70, 77–78
Mortensen, C., 141, 144

natural science, 1, 2
natural unity, 42
nature of intentionality, xvii
nature of numbers, xvii
nature of time, xvii
natures, 57–60
neglected views, x–xi

Nerlich, G., 91, 93, 97
neutral monism, 22–24
Newton, I., 57, 62, 75, 85, 90
nominalism, 51. *See also* resemblance nominalism
non-contradiction, xvi–xvii, 16, 129–31, 133, 134, 136–38, 141, 142, 144, 145
non-existent thing, 20

Ockham, W., ix, xiv, 18–19, 26–29, 51; to Aquinas's criticism of science of being, 18–19; concept of being, 26–30
order relations, 67–68
origin of ideas, xii–xiii

particulars, 51–54, 61–62. *See also* universals
perception, 44–45
perception are true, 3–5
persistent beings/things, 8–10
phenomenology arguments, xvi
Philoponus, J., xv, 83, 97, 118, 119, 146; displacement argument, 86; three-dimensional space, 84–86, 95, 96
philosophy, x–xi
Physics, 1, ix
Plato, 4, 7–11, 35, 50, 61; ancient world, 117; view of being, 9–10
Plato's *Theaetetus*: Cratylus, 9, 10, 132–34; Protagoras's relativism, 9, 16, 132–33
Politis, V., 47, 63, 144

powers and liabilities, 37, 39–40
predictable behaviour under ideal conditions, 49
presence of essence, 135
Priest, G., 144
properties, x; accidental properties, 11; causes of, 10; essential properties, 11
property of being, 19–21
propositional function, 21
Protagoras, xiii, 3–5, 9–11
Protagoras's view of being: beliefs are true, 3–5; criticism, 4–5; explanation, 3

re-identifiable individual, 43–44
relationism, 85, 88, 89, 93; argument against, 93–96; congruent counterparts, 94, 95; incongruent counterparts, 94, 95
relations: Aristotelian view, 65–66; Armstrong's view, 71–73; causal powers of interaction, 75–76; change of place, 65–66; conceptual vs. material necessity, 76; external relations, 66–67, 70, 75, 78–79; Heil's view, 75–76; internal relations, 71–73, 76; logic of, xv; Lowe's view, 73–75; monadistic theory, 68–69, 73–76; monistic theory, 69–70, 77–78; obscurantism, 70; order relations, 67–68, 79; powers and liabilities, 75–76; as properties, 65–66; relational truths, 73; Russell's view, xv, 66–70; spatial relations, 66; substance and attribute, 68–69; true relational statements, 78; truth-maker, 71
resemblance nominalism, 52
Russell, B., xiii, xiv, xv, 8, 20–26, 52, 54, 58, 66–73, 77–79, 100, 107, 108, 112; Armstrong's critique, 71–73; criticism, on being, 19–21, 30; monadistic critiques, 73–78; monistic theory, 69–70; solution, 21–26
Russell view of relations: explanation, 66–70; monadistic critiques of Russell, 73–76; monistic critiques of Russell, 77–78

Saint Andrew, 14
science, 1
scientific laws, xiv
shared essence, 50–51
Simplicius, 101, 113
Sklar, L., 97
Socrates, 34
sorites paradox, 139, 140
space: anti-realism about, xv; as emptiness, 82; material objects, xv–xvi; nature, xv–xvi; Philoponus's arguments, xv. See also Philoponus, J.; Zeno's paradoxes, xv–xvi. See also Zeno's paradoxes
spatial substantivalism: Euclidean geometry, 91–93; General Theory of Relativity, 92, 93,

97; identity of indiscernibles, 86, 89, 91; principle of sufficient reason, 86–89; Riemannian geometry, 92; thought experiment, Henri Poincaré, 89–91, 95
standard account of contraries and contradictories, 131
substance, xiv; being of things, 9–10, 15; criticisms, 43–44; and essence, 35–36; form of a thing, 35–36; identity, 34; primary substance, 34
substratum, 9–10
supernatural entities, beliefs about, 5
synchronic being, 134
systematic study of being, 17

Treatise of Human Nature, 19
truth-maker, 33, 71, 73–76, 130

units of reality, 33
unity and continuity, 37–38, 41–42
universals, xiv; arguments against, 60–62; categorical properties, 56–57; disposition, 54–55; exact resemblance, 52, 54; existence of, 52–53; idealisation, 62; immanent universals, 61, 62; internal relations, 54; law-likeness, 53, 62; law of nature, 53, 56. *See also* law of nature: multiplication of entities, 61–62; particulars, 52–54, 61–62; property, 20; resemblances, 52–54; responses to arguments for, 53–54
universal truth, xvi; beliefs are true, 4

Xenophon, 117, 118

Zeno's paradoxes, xv–xvi; dichotomy, 100, 101, 108, 109; material objects, components of, 111, 112; multiplication of entities, 110; paradox of plurality, 100–103, 108; paradox of the arrow, 101, 107; points in succession, 110; zero-sized instants, 107–11

About the Author

George Couvalis was a senior lecturer in philosophy at Flinders University in South Australia. He held previous positions in philosophy at the University of Adelaide, South Australia, and at the University of New South Wales. He is the author of two monographs: *Feyerabend's Critque of Foundationalism* and *The Philosophy of Science, Science and Objectivity*. He has published articles on the philosophy of science, the philosophy of law, social philosophy and Greek philosophy. His principal interests are the philosophy of Aristotle and the history and philosophy of science.